RELIGIOUS EDUCATION 1944-1984

CONTRIBUTORS

DAVID AYERST, C.B.E., M.A. *Formerly Staff Inspector, Department of Education and Science*

LIONEL ELVIN, M.A. *Director of the University of London Institute of Education*

FREDERICK HILLIARD, B.D., PH.D. *Reader in Religious Education, University of London*

THE REV. ROY LEE, M.A., D.PHIL. *Fellow of St Catherine's College, Oxford and Chaplain of Nuffield College, Oxford.*

HAROLD LOUKES, M.A., J.P. *Reader in Education, University of Oxford*

W. ROY NIBLETT, B.A., B.LITT. *Professor of Education and Dean of the Institute of Education, University of London*

THE REV. DENNIS NINEHAM, B.D. *Regius Professor of Divinity in the University of Cambridge*

MARY PARNABY, M.A., B.ED. *Dean of Women Students, Moray House College of Education, Edinburgh*

F. LINCOLN RALPHS, M.SC., LL.B., PH.D. *Chief Education Officer, County of Norfolk*

THE RT. REV. AND RT. HON. ROBERT STOPFORD, P.C., C.B.E., HON. D.C.L., D.D., M.A. *Lord Bishop of London. Chairman of the Church of England Board of Education*

THE REV. ALEXANDER WEDDERSPOON, M.A., B.D. *Lecturer in Religious Education, Institute of Education, University of London*

RELIGIOUS EDUCATION

1944 - 1984

EDITED BY

A. G. WEDDERSPOON

London
GEORGE ALLEN & UNWIN LTD
RUSKIN HOUSE MUSEUM STREET

PRINTED IN GREAT BRITAIN
in 10 point Juliana type
BY WILLMER BROTHERS LIMITED
BIRKENHEAD

CONTENTS

INTRODUCTION

ALEXANDER WEDDERSPOON

Section 25 of the 1944 Education Act states that '... The school day in every county school ... shall begin with collective worship on the part of all pupils in attendance at the school', and that '... religious instruction shall be given in every county school ...'

By these clauses, for the first time in English history, all county schools were legally required to provide for the religious education of their pupils. The rights of parents to withdraw their children from both the worship and the instruction were carefully protected by a conscience clause. The rights of teachers were similarly protected.

In 1954, the Institute of Christian Education[1] produced a report, *Religious Education in Schools* (N.S. and S.P.C.K.), to assess the working of the religious education clauses of the Act after the first ten years. This was mainly a factual review of the situation in the schools—organization of teaching; content of teaching; Agreed Syllabuses in use; staffing; examinations, etc.

In 1964 those of us responsible for the teaching of religious education in the Institute of Education in the University of London felt that the time had come for a further assessment of the situation. On sounding the opinions of a number of competent educationalists throughout the country we discovered that our views were very widely shared. Indeed we were made

[1] Since merged with the SCM in schools, the YMCA, and the YWCA to form the Christian Education Movement.

9

conscious of a sense of urgency for three main reasons, theological, educational and cultural.

The mood of 1964 was very far removed from that of 1944. In theological studies, all appeared to be in flux. In 1944 the 'image' of the Christian theologian was William Temple, Archbishop, scholar, moralist, educationalist. In 1964 the 'image' of the Christian theologian was John Robinson, Bishop of Woolwich. This was by no means without its implications for religious education. The publication of *Honest to God* in 1963 was followed—as is well known—by a deluge of other books, pamphlets and articles. *Images Old and New*, by the Archbishop of Canterbury; *Up and Down in Adria*, by Professor E. L. Mascall; *Four Anchors from the Stern*, by Professor A. Richardson and others; *The Secular Meaning of the Gospel*, by Dr P. Van Buren—and so on. The result of all this unaccustomed theological turmoil was, in the public mind, an unhappy ambivalence. Whereas on the one hand it certainly appeared that Christian theologians seemed to be grappling with the real questions men sought to ask, on the other it was depressingly obvious that the same theologians had no very clearly agreed answers to give. With what came to be called the 'New Theology' there also came to be associated the 'New Morality'. Publications such as *Towards a Quaker View of Sex* and Canon D. Rhymes' *No New Morality* appeared to give the impression that even much traditionally accepted Christian moral teaching was in question. The essays published in *Moral Education in a Changing Society*, edited by Professor W. R. Niblett, 1963, illustrated the sense of change, tension, and insecurity of principle. With so many foundations seeming to be shaken, the plight of the religious education teacher in school can be imagined. Many had to struggle day by day with critical sixth formers who gathered from television and the Press just enough about the New Theology and the New Morality to misunderstand both.

1964 also revealed some clear signs of questioning dissatisfaction within the field of religious education itself. The publication of Dr R. Goldman's book, *Religious Thinking from Childhood to Adolescence* aggravated the doubts many teachers of young children had long felt about the effectiveness of much of the religious education in the junior school. Mrs D. Dewar's book *Backward Christian Soldiers* suggested a depressing picture of almost total failure in the schools. These books came on top of much previous work of a critical kind, such as Sir Richard Acland's *We Teach Them Wrong*, and Harold Loukes' *Teenage Religion*. Those of us who were in close contact with the schools realized that these publications raised questions which were bound to concern practising teachers of religious education.

Education cannot, however, be separated from its cultural environment. All these strains and doubts have to be seen against a wider canvas. The religious education clauses of the Education Act passed into law at a time of high national purpose and idealism. The year 1944 saw the Invasion of Europe, the crusade of liberation. Great Britain was still great in military power and international prestige. It was a time of statesman-like planning and of national reconstruction. 1964 saw the dreariest of all General Elections fought over a few shibboleths of economics, totally unillumined by any glimpse of wider national vision. As Dean Acheson correctly observed, England had lost an Empire but had not yet found a role. At the time of President Kennedy's assassination an American research student working in London remarked, 'I feel as if I have been disinherited.' What contemporary British national leader could evoke such a reaction? In a leading article on the state of the nation twenty years after the end of the war in Europe, *The Times* remarked, 'Bafflement, uncertainty, a lack of any national consensus of opinion hang over many things.' There was a staleness and a flatness about the English scene, an easy acceptance of sophisticated cynicism. Night by night television spoke with the 'thin and acid voice of ridicule'.[1] It

[1] Spencer Leeson: *Christian Education*, Chapter 4, (Longmans).

was a climate in which the various secularist organizations found a readier following, especially in the universities. Optimistic rationalism had enjoyed but little vogue in the days of Buchenwald and Belsen. Religion and education cannot be separated from their contemporary culture and neither religion nor true education flourish in the rank soil of contented worldliness.

In thinking about this whole problem we realized that the first essential was a serious re-examination of the place of religion in education with particular reference to the educational justification for the teaching of religion in the county schools. A considerable debt of gratitude is owed to the Hibbert Trustees who decided to devote the Hibbert Lectures, 1965, to the subject. These lectures were delivered at two university centres in England by Dr F. H. Hilliard, Reader in Religious Education in the University of London; Sir Desmond Lee, Headmaster of Winchester College; Professor W. R. Niblett, Dean of the University of London Institute of Education; and Professor E. G. Rupp, Professor of Ecclesiastical History in the University of Manchester. They are published under the title *Christianity in Education*, by Allen & Unwin, and form an essential complement to this volume.

Restatement of principle, however essential, is nevertheless not by itself adequate in the practice of education. A re-examination of the situation in schools and training institutions was also seen to be necessary. In making further plans we were very conscious that the Education Department of the British Council of Churches had embarked on an extensive factual enquiry into religious education financed by the Gulbenkian Foundation and under the direction of a Committee of which the Chairman is Mr D. G. O. Ayerst, CBE, MA. We were most concerned to supplement and not to supplant this most valuable enquiry.

Educational research can be done in a variety of different ways, by questionnaire, written reports, examination of statistics, and so on. But education is essentially a human process;

the interaction of living personalities upon one another. We therefore decided to gather together a selected group of men and women engaged in the day to day work of religious education at various levels of the educational system. We sought to find what was uppermost in their minds, what were their hunches, moods, feelings and ideas about religious education after twenty years. What were their professional frustrations, satisfactions, and disappointments. This took place at a study conference held in London in April 1965, and this book is the report of the proceedings.

Chapter I to X consist of the lectures and addresses presented to the conference.

Chapter XI is an edited summary of the main conclusions and recommendations reached by the members of the conference in their group discussions, followed by a section of editorial comment.

The aims of the conference were:

1. To discover what were the aims, hopes and intentions of those who drew up the religious education clauses of the 1944 Act, and to consider how far these aims have been fulfilled.

    (Lord Butler kindly submitted a written statement outlining his intentions in this respect in 1944. Archbishop Lord Fisher gave a prolonged interview to the editor outlining what in his view were the intentions of the ecclesiastical negotiators in 1944. Both Lord Butler's statement and Archbishop Lord Fisher's remarks are incorporated in the opening chapter by Professor W. R. Niblett.)

2. To make some assessment of the strengths and weaknesses of religious education in the primary and secondary schools.

    (It should be noted that Chapters III and IV were planned by Mr Loukes and Mr Ayerst in consultation and to this extent should be read together.)

3. To make some assessment of the present situation in the training of teachers for religious education.
4. To consider the influence of the Ecumenical movement on Christian education in England.
5. To consider contemporary movements in psychology and theology and their bearing on religious education.
6. To consider the standpoint of the secular humanist, who often shares with the Christian educator a concern for the effective moral education of young people.
7. To outline some of the main needs and priorities of religious education in the next twenty years.

We fully realized that this represented an exceedingly ambitious programme, and that these themes could not possibly be dealt with in detail. Each one of them could have merited extensive independent treatment. Yet we believed the basic need of religious education to be sane and statesmanlike thinking about centralities and this is what we sought to achieve. This report must therefore be taken for what it is. It does not pretend to be a meticulous and detailed enquiry. It is a human document, giving the ideas, thoughts and opinions of men and women who are professionally engaged in religious education and who care about it very deeply indeed.

Editor's Acknowledgements

I should like to thank the Hibbert Trustees for their generous financial grant, without which the study conference could not have taken place. The concern and interest of Dr H. Stewart Carter, Secretary of the Trustees was a constant encouragement.

I should like to thank Professor W. R. Niblett for much shrewd counsel, often at inopportune moments.

I should like also to thank Dr F. H. Hilliard whose painstaking assistance at every stage contributed so materially to the success of the conference, and to whose personal kindness and magnanimity I owe so much.

CHAPTER I

THE RELIGIOUS EDUCATION
CLAUSES OF THE 1944 ACT
Aims, Hopes and Fulfilment

W. ROY NIBLETT

'Towards the end of the war,' writes Lord Butler, in the statement he has sent us, 'the feeling was widespread among many sections of the community that in any future measure of educational reform, religious instruction—and in the normal case Christian instruction—should play a larger part in the education of a child. The introduction to the section on religious education in the White Paper on Educational Reconstruction of 1943 refers to it in these terms:

> There has been a very general wish, not confined to representatives of the Churches, that religious education should be given a more defined place in the life and work of the schools, springing from the desire to revive the spiritual and personal values in our society and in our national tradition. The church, the family, the local community and the teacher—all have their part to play in imparting religious instruction to the young.

'My general aim and intention in framing the clauses dealing with religious education in what became the Education Act of 1944 was to recognize formally this special place of religion in education. In particular I was concerned to give effect, so far as practicable, and as part of a wider-ranging settlement acceptable not only to all the denominations with their differing interests but also to the other partners in the public education system, to what were known as the Archbishops' five points, put forward in 1941 in a general statement by the three Anglican Archbishops on the need for Christian education. These were that

   (i)   religious instruction should be given in schools to all children, subject to a conscience clause;

  (ii)   the school day should begin with a collective act of worship;

 (iii)   religious instruction should not be confined to particular periods of the school day;

 (iv)   agreed syllabus instruction should be open to inspection; and

  (v)   religious knowledge should be included as a subject for the Teacher's Certificate.

'I know that during the debates some doubts were expressed about the wisdom of making religious instruction and the corporate act of worship a specific requirement of the Act (subject of course to the right of withdrawal). But these doubts sprang, I think, mainly from the thought that it was unnecessary to make compulsory something in this field which was in practice universal, and it is fair to say that they did not represent any hesitation in the minds of most members about the principle that there was in the general education of all children a vital role for religious education.'

I

What I have to say, following this statement, will fall into three parts. First, I want to say something more about the background conditions that led to the religious clauses of the Act—which undoubtedly regard religious worship and knowledge as powerful, potential educators of the nation. Then I want to speak briefly about some of the foreground factors which led to the acceptance of this particular embodiment of Christian hopes. In the second half of my talk, I am going to ask to what extent these aims and intentions have so far been realized.

Nobody starting from scratch would ever have thought up the religious clauses of the 1944 Act. That is certain. But in human life we never do start from scratch: there is always a past within the present that affects what can happen. The clauses as they stand are to be read with an understanding of what had gone before: they are replete with history. It is not for me now, even in the form of a background sketch, to give a résumé of the struggles of centuries. I do not want to go back much further than the war years. The clauses themselves are an investment of the hopes for religious education of many Christians in the early forties, tempered by a sense of the possibilities. How far could one go at that time in a common policy for education which was to carry with it the denominations, the teachers and public opinion? The chances of the religious settlement of the 1944 Act working during the post-war years were much enhanced by the courage, optimism and depth brought by the war itself.

It is difficult for us now to recapture the spirit of that time. Those were years shot through with fear and determination. In the disturbance of men's minds and hearts, profound convictions which are normally unconscious came to the surface. There were moments for many people when they were aware that religion was a heritage they valued. At this level, religious belief was felt as something that bound the nation together rather than dividing it. Might it not help to knit society more closely into one fabric and be able to give men strength to face the tasks ahead? So, at any rate, it seemed at the time. 'The war,' says the White Paper on *Educational Reconstruction* from which Lord Butler has already quoted, 'has revealed afresh the resources of character of the British people—an enduring possession that will survive all the material losses inevitable in the present struggle.'[1] In his broadcast speech of 21st March 1943 Winston Churchill referred to religion as the 'fundamental element in school life'. He welcomed the progress

[1] *Educational Reconstruction*, page 3, paragraph 1.

B

made by all the religious bodies 'in freeing themselves from sectarian jealousies and feuds while preserving fervently the tenets of their own faith'.[1] Notice that word 'fervently'. It strikes us now with some suspicion. To the modern ear 'fervently' carries with it an undertone of doubt, of the whipping up of resources that are themselves under strain. But it had no such burden as Churchill used it.

Clearly, during those years of sweat and toil there was little that could actually be done to build new schools or colleges, even to replace the slums from which the evacuees poured, carrying their lice. Men were able to construct precious little that took physical resources. But in the mind they could create a new era; and the time invited them to cast their hopes forward. They could imagine, they could plan, and what a relief it was to do so! 'We believe,' said the Norwood Report of 1943, 'that education cannot stop short of recognizing the ideals of truth and beauty and goodness as final and binding for all times and in all places as ultimate values.... The recognition of such values implies, for most people at least, a religious interpretation of life.'[2] The idealism of the Fleming Report, the even bolder reformism of McNair, the grandly structured Education Act of 1944 itself, were all products of these years. Here were springboards on which to dance; from which to leap into the future. The religious settlement of the 1944 Act has to be seen as part of this whole movement; the religious clauses, which seem to some not altogether in keeping with the 1960s, simply take it for granted that there is enough religion and enough Christianity in the country for them to be practicable. For the truth is that the Act assumed that schools were, as Churchill said, apprised of the importance of religious education; and that one could rely upon the fact that England, and the Western world, were fundamentally Christian. You cannot

[1] *The Times*, March 22, 1943. Cf. Marjorie Cruickshank, *Church and State in English Education, 1870 to the Present Day*, London, 1963, page 160.

[2] *Curriculum and Examinations in Secondary Schools*, page viii.

give religious instruction in schools regularly to all children so that it matters unless there are enough teachers not merely able but willing to give it. You cannot hope to begin every school day with collective worship that is to be real unless there are many teachers who will be propagandists, even if silent ones, for that worship instead of propagandists, even if silent ones, against it. The religious clauses of the Act take such a background of faith and intention for granted.

There is little doubt that these provisions of the Act had the backing both of the teachers and of public opinion. From most schools, it is true, the religious clauses asked for little more than what they were already doing, though they made its doing less haphazard, more interdenominational. And it was partly because of this, no doubt, that teachers in general were behind the clauses. But at the time they were ready for a movement further in this direction rather than the opposite. Early in 1944 Mass Observation published the result of a survey of teachers' views on religious education. The representative sample they took of some 1,900 teachers from primary and secondary schools of varied types showed 90 percent of teachers to be in favour of religious education in State schools, and 71 percent to be opposed to merely denominational instruction in such schools.[1]

It was because Mr Butler (as he then was) had the support of the general public, of a large proportion of the churches, and of the majority of the teachers, that he was able to get agreement that non-denominational morning worship and regular religious instruction should henceforward be legally compulsory, not only permissive. To many, it could not have been religious sensibility which disposed them to close with the offer, though that was not altogether absent. There were at least two other impelling influences to make the religious clauses acceptable. One of these was the powerful connection in men's minds between Christianity and democracy itself. As Rosalind

[1] *Times Educational Supplement*, March 11, 1944.

Strachan has pointed out, one of the threads running through all the debates on the Education Bill in Parliament was the idea that we must teach people to be democrats and to know why they believe in democracy. 'During the previous thirty years,' she writes, 'three vigorous secular creeds had grown up, Nazism, Fascism and Communism, and throughout the discussions on the Bill Britain was at war with Nazi Germany and Fascist Italy. The war was seen as a clash of ideologies. To some it was a war between Nazi and Christian, but to most it was a war between totalitarianism and democracy. Therefore, people were forced to ask themselves what was the basis of this democratic tradition for which so many men had fought and died. And to the majority Christian ethics seemed to be the basis of British democracy. If it was the moral and spiritual strength of the churches which was the sustaining influence in the country during the war, and if this was the foundation on which the democratic tradition was built, then it was vital that the children of the nation should learn about the Christian faith in order that they, as citizens of the future, might have the necessary moral fibre to uphold the democratic way of life if ever it were threatened in a similar way.'[1]

This association of the Christian religion with the cause of democracy was one background factor which helped to secure a more widespread acceptance of the religious clauses than they might otherwise have had. Another was the way in which intelligent public opinion had been influenced by the interest Christians were so obviously taking in social questions. This then was no other-wordly religion : it was relevant, up-to-date, one in which the squabbles of the denominations of which the man in the street was tired were overcome by their common concern for national and social betterment. The Oxford Conference of 1937 on Church, Community and State saw leading Christians of many types hammering out the principles for which the west could stand; the Malvern Conference of 1941

[1] From an unpublished thesis by Mrs Rosalind Strachan.

was about industry and daily living. *The Christian News Letter* week by week challenged thoughtful laymen to see the connections between religion, conduct and national policy.

Who shall say exactly whence a fresh wind of ideas originates? But of its power once it blows to bring life to many minds there can be no doubt. People not conscious of a debt to J. H. Oldham, or the ecumenical movement, or to William Temple, may all the same owe them much.

Temple, however, was not merely a powerful background influence; he was a large foreground figure too in the negotiations which led to the fashioning of the religious clauses of the 1944 Act themselves. His appointment as Archbishop of Canterbury in 1942, the same year as that in which the British Council of Churches was constituted under his leadership, symbolized the victory of the interdenominational spirit. The discussion and examination of what was possible which went on before the clauses themselves were defined and accepted must have involved thousands of Englishmen and women, but the actual negotiators were chiefly Butler, Chuter Ede, Temple, Fisher (then Bishop of London), J. S. Whale, Scott Lidgett, and in some matters Cardinal Hinsley and later Archbishop Griffin. The embodiment of hopes and tendencies within defined legislation is a task calling for energy, persistence, ability to compromise. But behind all those must be sensitiveness to the direction in which the public mind is moving. Negotiators are the representatives of thinkers and feelers. They need not themselves be conscious of all the forces which move them nor need they be able to define in percentage terms the proportions of each. But they must permit the cross-currents to flow within them and if they are to be successful must embody as much of the vision as they can in the formulae they finally agree to.

Cold and legal as the religious clauses of the Act may appear (the clauses of any Act which seemed otherwise would be bad ones), they certainly contain idealism. Take, for instance, that central enactment, that the religious instruction in county schools shall be given in accordance with an agreed syllabus

adopted for the school ... [which] shall not include any cate-
chism or formulary which is distinctive of any particular
denomination'.[1] What battles are ended in the word 'agreed',
what a laying down of weapons in such abandoning of
denominational particularism! In fact, the church negotiators
—or at any rate the Protestant ones—needed to spend relatively
little time on inter-church disagreements. We have been assured
by Lord Fisher[2] that though most of the discussions which the
delegation from the Protestant churches had with Mr Butler
related to the theological content of an agreed syllabus, their
aims were educational, not ecclesiastical. 'Willie Temple and I
were both schoolmasters,' he said, 'that tells you all you need to
know.' He repudiated the idea that there was any bargaining
regarding the introduction of compulsion. The Church delegation felt that this was the only way to ensure that religious
education would still be taken seriously by the schools in the
post-war era. They saw the lack of staff qualified to teach
religious instruction as the greatest difficulty. But in 1944 they
hoped that this position would improve.

It may well seem to us now that in the negotiations leading
to the Act, too much weight was given to the avoidance of the
danger of denominational strife. It is easy to be of that opinion
today, when the last twenty years have seen such a rapid
rapprochement between the churches, even of late between
Catholic and Protestant believers. But the danger seemed real
enough in 1944—only seven years from Edinburgh[3] and four
years before Amsterdam had even happened.[4]

The first conviction of the negotiators, and the England
which, as we have seen, was in general behind them, was that
education must have a religious base and that the Act should
acknowledge this. There is no mention of Christianity in its
pages but the intention was, to quote Chuter Ede's words, that

---

[1] *Education Act 1944*, Section 26, paragraph 1.
[2] In an interview with the Editor.
[3] Where the Conference on Faith and Order was held in 1937.
[4] Where the World Council of Churches was inaugurated in 1948.

our 'children shall have a grounding in the principles of the Christian faith as it ought to be practised in this country'. As one of the most percipient American commentators upon the scene has pointed out, the Act gives religion a much enhanced status within the educational enterprise. Compulsory worship and instruction, freedom of time-tabling for religious teaching, the fact of inspection, all mean that religion is placed more nearly on a par with the rest of the curriculum than ever before.[1]

The expectation undoubtedly was that religion as a school activity would be upgraded. In the opening period of worship religion was formally acknowledged as something different from and more than instruction; though it was not to be an attempt to initiate a school into beliefs about God it was to orientate a young community so that it looked upon prayer and praise as natural, daily activities, recognized by the State as in every school normal and desirable.

In the period of religious instruction, the hope was that it would be possible to venture outside the safe harbour of Old Testament text and New Testament text. And the hope was founded upon the actual existing content of agreed syllabuses already in use before 1944. Dr Basil Yeaxlee, writing in *The Year Book of Education* for 1951, could survey the aim and content of these and later agreed syllabuses in this way:

> The courses are planned to help children to gain during the period of their school life, taken as a whole, an understanding of the whole Bible in outline with, of course, a more detailed knowledge of the Gospels and of the life and teaching of Jesus: an understanding of those truths which all Christian Churches regard as the vital elements of the Christian faith proclaimed in the New Testament and affirmed in the historic Apostles' and Nicene Creeds: some knowledge of the Church, the Christian ministry, and the Sacraments as these are described in the New Testament, and

[1] Cf. Gordon S. Lee: *Teachers' College Record*, Vol. 56 (1954-5), page 322.

the growth of the Church in the world from the first century to the twentieth: the application of Christian teaching to daily personal conduct and social relationships: and (for the sixth form) discussion of such questions as religion and science, Christianity and non-Christian religions, Christian ethics and social problems, and the like. Above all, the syllabuses provide help not only in the conduct of the daily act of worship required in all schools, but in the teaching of children at every stage in their development what worship means, and how they may practice it, personally and corporately.[1]

This is a brimmingly inclusive reading of the content of agreed syllabuses but the hope of the Act was undoubtedly that syllabuses should *not* be confined to the content of the Bible and that they should give scope for moral teaching. One of the basic hopes indeed was that moral education would result from the religious knowledge period and what Bishop Cockin has referred to as 'the moral wastage of the war years'[2] thus be made good.

II

How far have the far-reaching aims and bright hopes which lay behind its religious clauses been realized in the two decades since the passing of the Act? Can we proceed to draw up some kind of balance sheet? That is difficult to do for hard evidence is scarce and I must necessarily rely a good deal upon hunch and impression.

I think that first we should note how different were the war years, when death was near by, from those that have followed. England and the west have become less anxious and more affluent; it has been discovered by many that the easiest way to keep people happy is to keep them superficial. Commercialism has become smoother, glossier and more opportunist. The pre-

[1] *Year Book of Education* (1951), pages 287-8.
[2] *Theology*, July 1965.

dominant temper has not been one to encourage deep searching of heart or mind. We have had only occasional incentives to keep in touch with our roots or our deeper feelings. Scientists and philosophers have taught us to be suspicious of emotion; becoming more educated has meant, by and large, becoming more intellectual, but not necessarily more in touch with ourselves. The war period may thus be seen perhaps as in some ways an interlude. The tendency towards accepting the secular as the normal which was already clear in the pre-war years has been resumed. Not merely Christianity, but religion in general appears to many men in our time not to have a future. And so, they say, whether with a sigh or with relief, let us make the best of things without it. If we can't live here, at least let us board here as happily as we may.

Such a settling down from the upthrust of the war years to the levels of a neutralist mood is bound to have its consequences in any attempt fully to implement the religious clauses of the Act. For schools were never more a part of society in general than they are in an age as open and frank as ours. The walls are down, or at least permeable. As Harold Loukes has said so vividly, 'Schools have widened their frontiers, and the frontiers of the world have moved towards the young, so that the issues of adult life—getting and spending, working and cheating, loving and lusting, warring and peacemaking—are no longer hidden by a curtain of "not before the children".'[1] What men and women are feeling or failing to feel, thinking or failing to think, can communicate itself to the young more quickly than ever. Adult or pseudo-adult programmes on TV are watched by children, and by the young adults into which, at an earlier and earlier age, our children grow. If too many parents only want their children to get some religion at school as a kind of insurance policy, though they don't believe in it themselves, the job we give the school in the matter becomes impossible. Compulsory religious education in a thoroughly agnostic society

[1] *Learning for Living*, September 1961, page 4.

would be a contradiction in terms. But it would be quite wrong to say that England in these last twenty years has become *thoroughly* agnostic. Does it not tend to be as superficial in its agnosticism as in its belief? Rather, I fancy, it is separated from the deep, central sources of faith and compassion within it. In so far as children come to identify religion with a set of remote events recorded in the Bible, the intention of the religious clauses of the Act has not, whatever the reason, been fulfilled.

So much for generalized reflection. Let me come down nearer to earth. What, much more specifically, are the credits and the debits of the clauses as they have actually worked out in practice?

One point on the credit side is that the activity which has gone on in compiling and revising agreed syllabuses has in itself been a factor in bringing the denominations closer together. Clergy and teachers, theologians and members of education committees of very different church allegiances have got to know and trust each other more in this finite task of finding what each could agree upon as a feasible syllabus.

Secondly, and especially in the last ten years, the desire to improve agreed syllabuses and make them more viable has encouraged ministers of religion and teachers alike to seek to understand more about the way in which children's minds work. We have come to realize how little in fact we know about the development of religious interests and capacities and have begun to consult the psychologists—incidentally to their profit as well as other people's. Dr Goldman's work is really a very early effort to help here, as he would be the first to agree.

There has been a considerable evolution in the agreed syllabuses produced since the Act was passed. Some have begun to stress the relevance of their material to the present day and to reckon more adequately with the critical ability of teenagers. The newest generation of syllabuses certainly contains more articles and notes than the ones they supersede. The Surrey syllabus of 1963 includes, for example, ten pages headed 'Some of the problems of religion and life', and there is lively material in it for the fourth and fifth year secondary course on 'The Christian in the Modern World'. The new Welsh syllabus, also dated 1963, proposes a leaver's course with questions that challenge the teacher as well as children to work out what they believe: 'In what sense is the Bible true? Can I be a Christian without going to church? Can I spend my money as I like?' The newest edition of the West Riding syllabus is, I understand, being produced in close consultation with Dr Goldman himself. In all this we are suggesting that it is not the teacher's job to avoid dangerous river crossings or difficult hillclimbs. It may still be right to criticize most syllabuses for being too bookish, out of touch with real children and real life, but it is tending to become at any rate rather less true.

Thirdly, the clauses have stimulated the production of more trained specialist teachers of religious knowledge than we had in this country twenty years ago. It was, for instance, quite rare then for a boys' grammar school to have any properly equipped teacher of scripture on its staff. Now that is much more common, as it also is in other grammar schools, comprehensive schools and secondary modern schools. It is true that the very availability of a specialist may enable everyone else to live the more contentedly in their little boxes and to observe without any striking of conscience the famous rule 'Leave it to him'. The specialist himself indeed may busily cultivate a garden of his own, teaching the subject in highly respectable, academic ways not unknown to yield satisfying results at 'O' level. All the same, by and large, the specialist teachers of the subject are among the most liberal and the best. And they should continue to be, as the Act contemplated, full-time, trained teachers. Australian experience of using clergy or ministers part-time to do this work does not offer a happy augury of the success of any such alternative. We must produce more specialist teachers but be more aware of the danger, which specialization emphasises, of separating religion from life and making it simply another subject.

Fourthly, there is no doubt that in Colleges and Departments of Education religious knowledge as a subject is taken more seriously and is taught by better equipped lecturers. Courses for teachers of the subject are provided in much greater numbers than before the Act by the Department of Education and Science, by Institutes of Education, by Extra-Mural Departments of Universities. And large numbers of teachers have attended these, showing abundant interest and seriousness.

Again, much more thought has been given to the conduct of worship at morning assembly for children of every age range since the passing of the Act than before it. The BBC has been an inspiration in this regard, and on many school days it has sent over the air programmes not merely helpful to the content of religious instruction lessons but frequent in their suggestion to teachers about how they might approach the subject themselves. Good new school hymn books and good books of prayers for schools have appeared more often in the last twenty years than in the previous twenty, though some bad ones have appeared too.

There are many more plusses to the credit of the religious clauses of the 1944 Act than I have mentioned. But it has to be acknowledged, whatever the causes, and I introduced this part of this lecture by suggesting some fundamental ones, that most children are not leaving school with even the minimum knowledge of religion and interest in it which those who saw the religious clauses safely packed into the Act would have hoped. We shall have much more definite evidence about this when the wide-spreading inquiry into the nature and future needs of religious education in this country now being carried out by the British Council of Churches has been published in two years' time.

But there is evidence that much tame and tepid teaching of religion in schools still goes on. The supply of teachers who vitally relate their teaching of the Bible to life is not big enough. And the churches, by and large, are not helping them enough. It is remarkably easy for children, or grown-ups, to forget anything taught them which seems useless or beside the point. Knowledge about religion is very different from knowledge of religion, which, almost certainly, can only be communicated by persons who themselves have a genuine faith, untidy though it may be. To settle for secularism anyway is much easier than to delve into the mind to discover what one really believes or what principles, if any, one would really go to the stake for.

It is because some humanists and some Christians have come to see that they are together in their desire for more robust and less sentimental thinking about moral principles that it is not impossible that, at any rate within this limited territory, they may be able to agree on a programme of moral education which might be desirable, in addition to agreed syllabus teaching. More than that: some Christians and some humanists might go a considerable way together in asking for a more open-ended approach to religious education itself, with the emphasis much more on genuineness in facing the difficulties of living and believing than in toeing lines. It is significant that the title of the magazine which used to be *Religion in Education* has become *Learning for Living*, and that by far the most widely read theological book of our time is called *Honest to God*.

The chief debit of the religious settlement of 1944 appears today perhaps as a certain—what shall I call it?—provincialism. The religious clauses are too much concerned, however understandably and forgivably, with preventing what now seem rather provincial struggles between churches. Do not the references to 'tenets' which are 'distinctive' of some 'particular religious denomination' bulk altogether too large in them? We are more aware than we were that Christianity is not to be confined within post-Reformation terminology, or even western forms of thought, let alone denominational particularism. The world is so much smaller than in 1944; the number of non-Christians in it so much larger than it was then; and the number of non-Englishmen so much more apparent to us.

A second debit which strikes us now is that the agreed syllabuses so much encouraged by the Act are too theological and historical in their preoccupation. Perhaps, we suspect, this is because after all it is easier to be agreed about much history and theology than what the answers are to many questions posed in 1965 by everyday and urgent life. Without any doubt the newer agreed syllabuses are improvements upon older ones. But, how far along this road have we come even yet? Not perhaps so very far. Maybe we cannot get as much help from the theologians in this matter as we could if their own training in college days had introduced them more often to the applications of their theology, had contained more sociology and consideration of the ethics of everyday life. But where does one start to break this circle? Through an Institute which brings schoolteachers and social thinkers in to teach the theologians or a Centre of a new kind in which the laity are helped to see what theology is really about? We greatly need more well-trained and more deep-thinking theologians, both clerical and lay. Can we indeed have agreed syllabuses of the kind most required until soundings have gone deeper and objections to Christian belief been dealt with at a profounder level of insight?—a level which only a struggle involving heart as well as head can produce. We are still on the wrong side of the eye of this needle, but maybe the answer when we get it will not consist either, in Eliot's words, in getting the contentment we wanted,

> Or in getting rid of what can't be got rid of,
> But in a different vision.[1]

The third debit of the religious clauses perhaps lies in their insistence upon the attendance at collective, daily morning worship of all pupils not withdrawn at the request of their parents.

[1] T. S. Eliot: *The Family Reunion*, Part II, Scene II.

In practice older pupils in a number of schools now are left to make the decision for themselves whether they shall attend, the points for and against having been thoroughly discussed; and, whatever the dangers, this is surely right. We do not compel attendance at worship in institutions of further or higher education, nor are we likely to do so if junior or sixth form colleges become more common, as a number of powerful social forces at present operating suggest that they will in the next twenty years.

In so far as the religious clauses encourage insincerity they are not helpful to a mature religion : of that we are becoming more and more aware. For intellectual honesty is one of the very keys to maturity of mind. At every stage of religious education we need freedom for the pupil to express his puzzlement and his problems of understanding. But if that is not to mean a bandying about of superficial difficulties, a lot must depend upon the extent to which school and classroom are places in which problems not answerable simply by information or logic can be brought into the open and really discussed.

The creation in a school of a climate in which profound questions can be asked is no easy task, especially in our own time. The degree of sincerity required is not likely to come unless there are at any rate occasional meetings between teachers and taught as full human beings, with the difference between fifteen and fifty acknowledged on both sides as the essentially minor thing it is.

'Boy,' said Keate, the famous headmaster of Eton early in the nineteenth century, 'you will believe in the Holy Ghost by five o'clock this afternoon, or I will beat you till you do.' We have no faith today in such an approach. But *any* attempt to compel belief or moral action is essentially open to the same accusation and I am not sure that the religious clauses of the 1944 Act are entirely free from a suspicion of it.

As children get older the concern of religious education must be less with adding to knowledge than getting them to examine their pre-suppositions about life and the nature of things. And that in honesty demands their own co-operation. The teacher, even the head of a school, must not often be on a pedestal. After all there is nowhere to step from a pedestal except off it. But such equality of standing ground is a hard test for us. Whether we are Christians or agnostics it can be too revealing of our own doubts and fallibilities. One of the brightest young university teachers I know said to me the other day, 'I am in favour of a purely intellectual education because I am not confident enough of my moral and personal position to be in favour of anything else.' Such lack of inward confidence is one of the fundamental difficulties of implementing the religious clauses in our time.

Yet there is no way through to a new confidence save one which reckons with more than the superficial. Part of the strength of the religious settlement of 1944, as I suggested to start with, sprang from the insight into ourselves that the war years brought. The implementation of the religious clauses of the Act must continue, but it must not get in the way of the search for a less merely conventional understanding of God. There are many who still lack any proper religious education in spite of the clauses and who under trial in early adolescence retort as it were: 'You're not the sort of God they brought me up to believe in.' And they stop going to church just to show him!

Every new truth begins in an astonishment. The essential truths in Christianity cannot arrive in us unless we have the openness of mind and heart to be astonished. Soon we shall only be able to accept many of the primary truths of the Bible if we boldly discard their wrappings. The religious clauses of the 1944 Act must not be allowed to prevent either honesty of mind or genuineness of feeling. In the years ahead we must obey them in much the spirit in which Beethoven observed so faithfully the rules of music—treating them as guides in principle, yes, but as our very humble obedient servants too.

CHAPTER II

RELIGIOUS EDUCATION IN THE PRIMARY SCHOOL

F. LINCOLN RALPHS

Religious education in the primary school is a wide theme having in mind the range of interest, age and ability of the children in primary schools, and the equally varied practice to be found in the several schools. Even so I cannot begin to deal with this topic without emphasizing the need to see the issues against the wider context of religious education and observance generally, and in the climate of religious opinion in the country as a whole. A comparative study of the religious education of young children in different countries throughout the world would make it plain that in this, as in many aspects of our educational system, this country is unique.

Professor Niblett, in his introductory lecture, has reminded us of the conditions which gave birth to the religious clauses of the Education Act of 1944 which for the first time made religious education a statutory duty. The whole Act was in many ways as much an act of faith as an act of Parliament. It set down, in the context of a war the outcome of which was still unknown, the basis of the faith that inspired our hope of victory. Basically it was the belief that some things are right and some are wrong and that in the end the right will emerge triumphant because we hold the view, however vaguely formulated, that man is not to be debased but liberated into freedom and destined to hold the dignity of one created in the image of God. It is this basic faith that still inspires scientific research, as for instance the ceaseless, confident, hopeful

33

research for the cure for cancer. No-one regards this faith as irrational. It is of the nature of man, peculiar to him and distinguishing him in nature, not merely in degree, from all other animal creation. This distinction tends to be blurred in an age that is more concerned with our association with the animal world than with our ascendency over it.

All education, and not only religious education, reflects in the last analysis the general conception of the nature and purpose of man. The State's education manifests the State's opinion and as this may change, legislation, in time, is made to reconcile the situation to conformity. So it was perhaps not unnatural that in the years of national adversity, when issues of right and wrong, and of good and evil, were brought into sharp focus as issues of life and death, the State expressed its earlier belief in religion in a formal way. Worship and religious teaching became a statutary element in the state school system. Adversity brought us quickly, and perhaps too fearfully, to an attitude of heart and mind that craved religion. Affluence less readily achieves this result. It is still harder for the rich man to acknowledge the Kingdom of God. And the riches may be intellectual as well as material.

Religious education in our technological age has to be seen against its social and scientific background and made relevant to it. All subjects suffer if taught out of context for all specialisms produce bias and blinkers, but in no subject is context more important than in religious education. Indeed some would argue that it is itself more context than subject. The student of mathematics might well pursue his studies in a society that was innumerate although he would be helped if his community recognized that two and two made four rather than five. He himself would need to hold this view inflexibly. Religion, which is essentially concerned with the way of life, similarly disintegrates when theory is divorced from practice; but when the two are reconciled it needs must permeate the environment. To a large extent it is true to say that the good teacher of religion is the good person 'Religion is caught not taught', and in no teaching is it more difficult to avoid the injunction 'follow me'. The state, in its own system of education, and ultimately of schooling, cannot escape this exemplary role. In 1965 the State is less sympathetic to organized religion than it was twenty-one years ago. It is less certain of what is right and wrong, less willing to pronounce on moral issues and the uncertainty encourages the growing sense of irrelevance. If the religious clauses of the Act remain unchanged in the next decade it may well be due more to this attitude than to the strong belief in their fundamental importance to the health of the nation.

This climate of opinion vitally affects religious education in the primary school which continues and augments the education given in the pre-primary stage at home. Few parents will enquire of schools as to the moral or spiritual welfare of their children. They are more eager for success in the eleven plus, or for its abolition if success seems doubtful. In the amoral society success is demanded not deserved. In the secondary school stage the five 'O' levels assume more importance than the pentateuch. The Bible will not often be seen at home, even more rarely will it be read. Christ will be an expletive as often as an example. Few children will see their parents on their knees except perhaps to adjust the television set which if they stay up long enough, and many do, will almost certainly find some justification to ridicule the religious faith they are taught in school. For some this has become a very profitable enterprise.

All this is perhaps not surprising in an age of scientific achievement. The scientist has tended to acquire, some would say usurp, the role of the priest. His obedience to law in the material world has yielded such rich rewards that the techniques of materialism have tended to obscure all others. We are inclined to become a quantitative society with mathematics rather than morals as our lingua franca. The new is so often the good that it may be confused with it and the old derided out of hand. Size is confused with significance and the normal with the desirable as the average becomes the datum. Only measurable phenomena are significant. In such a context the arts lie in confusion and religion which is age-old and traditionally the trust of the remnant, is generally at discount. This is the difficult apathetic atmosphere in which our teachers of religious instruction are called to work. It says much for their quality that in many primary schools the instruction and the worship is often excellent and at times inspiring.

Comparatively little research on scientific lines has been carried out into the nature of the religious experience of young children. The Study and Research Committee of the Institute of Christian Education as far back as 1936 produced a few pamphlets, subsequently revised and reprinted. From these and other comparable documents I should like to take a few statements at random. For the religious education of children under seven 'no formal instruction need be given for the children under seven learn not by being taught but by action and enquiry'. 'It is a serious error in the treatment of young children to try to promote good behaviour by putting children upon their honour. At this early age a child has no sense of honour.' 'It is of the utmost importance to recognize that religion and morality, in the full adult understanding of these terms do not enter into the experience of the child under seven.' 'Misbehaviour should always be treated in a calm and matter of fact way and dismissed and forgotten as soon as possible. The child must not be expected to feel guilty nor must he be allowed to find that by misbehaviour he can disturb adults.'

All these excellent comments assert the difference, but do not define in precise and scientific terms the nature of the difference, between a child's approach to religion and the approach of the more mature adult. More recently Dr Goldman has accumulated some interesting material in this field, but even here I feel some doubt as to the wisdom of drawing conclusions. In so much modern research one is left with the feeling that answers are more related to questions and questions are often contaminated by preconceptions. I suspect that most findings will confirm the view that the character of the teacher is the most potent element in the teaching of religion to young children. This is not to suggest that the teacher can with impunity avoid the intellectual requirements or the special training required for other disciplines. It does mean that for him, more than for most, he must be aware that he is teaching children rather than his subject. To this end I believe it to be most important to ensure that those who specialize in religious education should have in their own lives a clear and considered sense of purpose, combined with a triumphant experience of life itself. It is not always apparent from the countenances of Christians that they are the recipients of good news and the face of the teacher is often the best visual aid in the classroom. The teacher of religious instruction should be the toughest, gayest, most energetic and least pious member of the school staff. Further he should be of the same intellectual calibre as the best of his colleagues, no less diligent in accepting and requiring standards. There is welcome recognition of this now in the General Certificate of Education papers in this field.

I had the great good fortune to prepare this talk in Jerusalem and by the Sea of Galilee in the company of many teachers who had come together to visit the Holy Land. I believe that a period of time in the Holy Land is almost essential to the train-ing of teachers who are to specialize in religious education in schools. It is a reflection of the lack of importance attached to this subject that this suggestion will cause some surprise to some education authorities. In our technological age we allow our language specialists to study abroad; we are able to afford for our science teachers well-equipped laboratories, we recog-nize that biologists and geographers must have their field studies and foreign travel. For our religious instruction specialist an up-to-date translation of the Bible, a film strip or a flannelgraph is all too often the limit of our provision, aug-mented maybe with a few other visual aids that are often over sentimental and effete.

No teacher who is familiar with the Holy Land at first hand

could happily continue the sentimental portrayal of an emasculated Jesus that every intelligent growing child must be expected to abandon even before he leaves the primary school. In an age that finds strength in realism and in a discipline that has a minimum of demonstrable actuality it is almost unforgiveable that so little is done to make use of an environmental experience that has for 2,000 years been remarkably preserved. There may be only a limited future for this. The speed boats on Galilee are already shattering the sabbath rest and the waterfront is being developed. Nazareth is fast becoming an industrial town. None the less the essential geography of biblical times remains and often one can walk into an environment little changed in many ways from that Christ knew. In this situation one may see in an instant the relevence of His comments to the local situation and the stupidity of their literal application elsewhere. Furthermore children, even young children, listen with added interest to the teacher who has been and seen. Local education authorities could do worse than subsidize such expeditions. Teacher training colleges and theological colleges should hasten to repair a serious ommission. And nowhere would the benefits be greater than in the primary school where the imagination can run riot without the restraint of authentic experience.[1]

But I must return more precisely to my theme. In general I would distinguish quite sharply the needs of the infants from those in the later ages of the junior school. The need of the

[1] Not least important in a visit to the Holy Land is the discovery that the organized churches have so built-in the 'Holy Places' as almost to exclude the spirit of Christ from them. To see the Holy Sepulchre in the crowd of a Good Friday struggle is almost to hear the echo of the cry 'He is not here'; but to walk beside the sea of Galilee in the early morning is almost to hear His voice still calling for fishers of man. This at least has been the experience of the groups of teachers I have been privileged to take to this unique and fascinating country. I think it is an encouragement to those who feel and find difficulty in securing co-operation between local church organizations and the schools' religious activities.

infant is essentially for security and affection which is found
at its highest in true religion. Where love is, God is. Let the
theological portrait painters be they honest to God or otherwise, take their talents elsewhere. They have little relevance to
infants. Love is God; that is all the infant child needs to know.
It might serve adults well to have a like philosophy, a rebirth
that extends charity to those who stumble. Modern humanism
is encouraged by the failure of religious persons to differentiate
the sinner from his sin, making no concession to the latter and
no condemnation of the former. It is the major part of the difficult task of religious instruction to show, and most
effectively by example to show, that for Christians human
relationships are founded on love. How difficult nowadays is it
even to use the word love which belongs to sacrifice and has
been misappropriated by sex.

If I venture a few words on infant worship I do so with great
diffidence. Very little is known about it. I believe the most
suitable place for worship is the place where love is most mani-
fest. The attitude should be reverent but not unintelligent.
Worship requires the complete dedication of all our talents. It
may be helpful for an adult to close his eyes to the distractions
that might hinder the concentration of his thinking in prayer.
It is not easy to know what goes on in the mind of the child
with his hands together and his eyes, for part of the time,
closed. It looks very nice to the adult but it may seem odd to a
child who for the most part is encouraged to open his eyes in
wonder. Wonder and worship are not very far apart. We must,
of course, try to discover what God means to the young child.
We must be careful as far as we can to avoid confusion. The well
tried method of the story is an appropriate method used by
Christ himself. If the story manifests love, and it should, it can
well be followed by a thankful prayer. Perhaps thank you is all
the religious training the child brings from home. In matters
of language I find it difficult to agree with those who seek to
restrict this to what is assumed to be wholly comprehensible to
the child. The Lord's Prayer can be learned at an early age, few

sentences can bear such repetition, few prayers continue
to challenge even the oldest and most wise. The parables, told,
even learned, in the language of the Bible (there is none better)
are surely part of worship, especially if again appropriately
enacted in costume or in mime. I would rather that our children were familiar with the words of Jesus Christ as recorded in
the Gospels than that they embarked on the tedious journeys
of St Paul with its attendant geographical interest in the Medi-
terranean. These sayings set in proper context would, I believe,
provide a framework which children would wish to fill in
rather than discard in their teens.

The recent report on Sunday schools which recorded the fall-
ing off in Sunday school attendance at the end of the primary
school stage should give us cause to re-examine our methods
and our content. More is needed than a revision of the agreed
syllabus. In this connection however I venture to advocate the
story of the historic Jesus as the starting point. He was with
His disciples a long time before they were asked to identify
Him. The thirty years in the carpenter's shop were as much a
part of His ministry as the three years of His preaching. He
begins as the Son of Man. Even His disciples walked a long
way with Him on the Emmaus road before they re-recognized
Him and He immediately vanished. With the hind-sight of
2,000 years I think we are in danger of starting at the end;
of writing holy on the Bible before we have read it.

The Bible must play an important part in religious instruction and I am a little disturbed by those who seem to wish to
leave this to a later, even a much later, stage. We need
of course to avoid the use of archaic language that is confusing.
This is no less true of our hymns. Children should not be left
wondering why a green hill did not have a city wall. The newer
translations are helpful but I think that the paraphrases of the
Phillips kind belong to the secondary rather than the primary
schools. They are excellent but possibly ephemeral. Stories from
the Bible rewritten for young children and generously illustrated range from the few that are good to the many that are

bad. Those that seek to explain the text are in general best avoided.[1]

Music is normally associated with school worship and in general this is improving in the primary school. None the less few religions have been required to survive the efforts of the incompetent in this field. The one finger on the keyboard of the piano at least a tone out of tune is still too often the counterpart of the mission harmonium. There is no reason to suppose that God welcomes imperfections in musical performance any more than He welcomes imperfections in human character. It is a sad fact that we are inclined to accept lower standards of efficiency in religious activity than we would tolerate elsewhere. The technological age brings new opportunities. Broadcasting and records can help. It must however be remembered that a television set, a radio or a tape recorder can be as disastrously defective as a piano that is out of tune. Local education authorities are coming round to the view that a service of technical assistance is needed in all schools. It should also be stressed that the primary schools can often make best use of these modern aids although, because the schools are often small, they may be denied them on grounds of expense. This is just one of the ways in which we fall into the error of thinking that primary education is of secondary importance and vice-versa. In so far as they include other than music, aural aids are likely to be more successful with juniors than

[1] Perhaps I speak with bias for I must confess that even St Matthew seems to me to be irritating in his enthusiasm to relate the actions of Christ to the Jewish prophesies. This seems to me to be as unfortunate and dubious as the attempt to interpret Our Lord's cry 'My God, My God why hast thou forsaken me?' as a meek recital of the 22nd psalm rather than the ultimate and complete identification of Himself with man in his lowest possible depth of despair, redeemed by His supreme act of faith in the commendation of His spirit into the hands of the Father. Surely it is significant that at that moment the veil of the temple was rent, from top, notice, to bottom. The Holy of Holies and the holy place were one in this final agonizing stage of His incarnation.

with infants. For the very young active participation is almost essential. We have of course to remember that some infant school teachers are a little nervous and inexperienced in this field. More might be done in college training and by local education authorities by in-service training in the use of modern equipment.

It is encouraging to see experiments in the use of modern music. It is part of a legacy from our organized church services that religious music seems dull to children. The churches themselves have realized this and the robust sentiments of many old hymns have got new vitality in more vigorous music, despite the cathedral organists. The truth is of course that both have their place and I have seen very young children enthralled in the music of the Festival of Carols recorded from King's College in Cambridge. Nor need religious music require static attention. We may dance, no less than make a joyful noise unto our God. We may worship with every instrument and with all our strength. It would be a misfortune if the school's religious activity contributed to the dichotomy of religious and secular life which had no part in the Christian faith but is rather a legacy from the Judaistic conception which our Lord desired to extend rather than continue.

With audio aids it is common to associate visual aids. In no aspect of religious instruction is there a wider range of material from the very many that are bad to the very few that are really good. I am little inclined to commend portrayals of Jesus which are all too often sentimental, sloppy and reduce rather than enlarge the image. He is a personal and individual Christ. We must see Him for ourselves. Films are often crudely inaccurate. Some reasonably accurate reconstructions are possible, as for instance, the temple, the typical synagogue, the traditional home. The classroom can be adapted to the latter. Eastern costume is easy to simulate. Many teachers brought back the genuine costume from the Holy Land.

There is now a substantial literature on the geographical, geological biological and ethnological aspects of the Holy Land which can guide teachers towards authenticity. The long flight of the Holy family to Egypt is capable of realistic reconstruction and impressive representation to the junior school. It should no longer be possible to discover the childish representation of the flight by aeroplane with Pontius the pilot. It is fatally easy to pick up glamourized and misleading images. The teacher must be at great pains to avoid these.

I have already indicated the central place which I would give to the Bible in religious education. If used unintelligently it is obviously defective. Its very divisions while facilitating reference generally confuse its message. Our treatment of it in reading fragments rather than as a related whole is also to be deplored.[1]

I have touched on only a few obvious elements in religious worship and instruction. I turn to the Act of worship in assembly. There may of course be problems of accommodation and withdrawal. I do not subscribe to the view that places of worship should be uncomfortable. To stand too long, to sit too uncomfortably is in no sense virtuous. I realize only too well the difficulties that have to be overcome. Dual use of space can be restrictive. It is also true that the assembly is a convenient but inappropriate occasion for rebuking the school or for making announcements about the dinner money. Dual use of time can be as unfortunate as dual use of space. Infants and juniors seem to me to require quite distinct treatment. The youngest could be allowed to leave so that from the beginning the juniors feel that religious instruction is for a maturing rather than an infant mind.

There is much merit in allowing the children to take an active part in any act of worship. I have often been surprised at the sensitivity and discernment displayed in prayers which children of ten or eleven years of age have composed. It is sometimes possible to make use of nearby church premises where these can be made available without restriction, and

[1] I commend to all teachers the Peake Lecture given by Professor T. E. Jessop, *On Reading The English Bible*, Epworth Press, 1958.

where they are conducive to worship. It is a valuable asset to see the inside of churches when they are not occupied by their normal congregations. Free access for small groups or individuals has value. It is a defect in our noisy school life that we are rarely able to provide a quiet spot where children can go, when they want to be alone and they often want to get away from the grouped activities of class organization. The growing spirit of co-operation between the denominations may allow a better use of facilities in churches than has so far been possible. It should also not be forgotten that the Christian church had its early origins in the open air. Admittedly the climate was more genial than our own; none-the-less I have sometimes felt sorry to see a school crowded together on the hot day (which we sometimes have in term time if not in vacations) when a nearby park which was part of the school grounds might have been a more agreeable venue. Religious activity of all kinds tends to ossify into patterns and moulds that acquire quite undue significance.

It might be appropriate to say a word about the relation of the Sunday school and the primary school since most Sunday school pupils are primary school children. It has been said that the most efficient Sunday school is the school run by the day school teacher. There is certainly need for better co-operation than now exists. Joint refresher courses might help. A school morning assembly in which parents took part might pave the way. More could be done in liasion with such bodies as the National Sunday School Union and the Christian Education Movement. The trend towards unity should help this. We can still find too many Sunday schools where the teacher's major achievement is to maintain order rather than advance spiritual insight.

In the secondary school field Professor Niblett has pointed out a common desire for more robust and less sentimental thinking about moral principles, and has encouraged the hope of an extension of agreed syllabuses to a programme of moral education. This has relevance in primary school work. No-one familiar with the current proceedings in juvenile courts will fail to recognize the urgent need for the establishment of moral foundations. Religious instruction has a proper part to play in this. No religion is potentially more suited than the Christian religion, the most materialistic of all religions and the one most concerned with good neighbourliness. It is a pathetic paradox that Christianity which, of all religions, offers the best climate for science, should, through the centuries, have in its ecclesiasticism been so often and so unnecessarily in conflict with science. Some look to the closing decades of this century for a reconciliation based on a truer humility and sincerity on both sides. The scientific humanist is frequently not far from the Kingdom of God.

In conclusion, and in general, I think it fair to recall the prophesy of Professor Alex Findlay that if the churches did not come together in the daylight they would huddle together in the cold night. The cold night may be approaching. Christianity is assailed and openly assailed not because its tenets have been proved to be untrue but because its disciples have been following too far off and its standards are too uncomfortable for a generation that confuses liberty and licence. The mystery of the resurrection is an offence to the materialistic rationalist and even theologians are prepared to give ground on this belief. Yet the historic evidence does not call for such accommodation to the climate of current scientific thinking. The thoughtful citizen is concerned lest having gained the capacity for men to encircle the earth they still lack the inspiration to inherit the earth. New philosophy has bred neither morality nor integrity competent to resolve the human situation. Those engaged in the religious education of children in primary schools may be concerned with a generation that may have perhaps a final opportunity for this endeavour. It is no small assignment.

The Ministry's *Handbook of Suggestions* published in 1959, devotes three times the space to the teaching of languages and to handicraft that it devotes to religious instruction. It is well that we should know how to make things; it is well that we should know how to converse with each other. But if in our talking and trading we have not love towards each other the obedience which has given emancipation in the material world will ironically, as from an earlier Eden, banish us to oblivion. The aim of religious education in the primary school is to discover and develop those potentials within the individual that contribute to a proper appraisal of the status of man—not seeking to excuse defects which we despair of the hope of redeeming. His standard of human nature, not ours, is the new salvation. The primary school is the best age to introduce this. The idea grows best in the genial climate of example.

CHAPTER III

RELIGIOUS EDUCATION IN THE SECONDARY SCHOOL

(a) *The Pupil's Response*

HAROLD LOUKES

The question I want now to raise is a question that Christians usually consider too shameful to ask: the question, What will Jones swallow? It is, indeed, a shameful question if it is taken to mean, How can we water down the distasteful drink of the Christian challenge so that men and women will take to it as to a 'smooth and friendly little wine' in the hope that they might become addicts without quite meaning to? For if, in the name of Christianity, we make addicts to smoothness and friendliness, then we blaspheme against the name. The Christian challenge is to roughness, the bitter roughness of the cross, and to unfriendliness, to the pain of leaving home and kin and friends for a place in the depths of Being where a man is, in an ultimate and agonizing sense, alone. Now about *this*, there can be no attempt at compromise. In the shadow of the cross, we do not ask, What will Jones swallow? Here, at the heart of the Christian experience, there is 'naught for your comfort'. And the search for a comfortable way of presenting this uncomfortable truth is a search for a lie.

But there is another sense in which the question What will Jones swallow? is not only a real question but a deeply Christian question, a loving question, full of tender concern for Jones, an assertion of his being and value. What we are asking here is the question, What *can* he swallow? What, being Jones—and that is our first stirring of love for Jones, that asking about his being—what, being Jones, can he understand, respond to, take hold of for himself? There is no compromise involved in taking *this* question seriously. The compromise, indeed, is the other way, for if we shirk this question, we declare that love is too much for us, that we are prepared to recite 'pure' Christian statements in unexceptionable language, but not to engage in a human dialogue, to wrestle naked, to traffic in the open market place with another human soul.

Now my question is a special, and specially urgent and challenging, form of this one: the question, What can Jones Minor swallow? It is a question that has become increasingly important in all educational thought during the 200 years since Rousseau. Children are not—we have now learnt to say—little pots to be filled with liquid learning, pint by painful pint, until they are full. Children are exploring animals who learn best what they see and touch, manipulate and perform for themselves. And so in our school studies we now plunge our children into a world of things, things with different lengths and weights and shapes and colours; and the teacher hangs back while the children make their own discoveries, and sometimes he pushes ahead and tells his children what to look for, but always, if he is any good, saying, in effect, Look, do you not see? And when dispute arises, the teacher, if he is any good, turns in the end to the 'things' themselves: the facts of the case. 'Do rivers run uphill? Do all metals expand equally when heated?' 'Well,' he says, 'let's see.' As A. B. Clegg put it the other day, 'We are finding that where children want to find out; where they do rather than see or hear; where it is thrilling and exciting; where they learn with confidence and enjoy free discussion, then this contributes to their mental metabolism.'

Now the storm that has hit religious education lately, and taken all our breath away, has come because we have just begun to attack it with this, the crucial educational question. In the old days—the good old days, some would sadly say— Christians used to bring up their children to religion by a set of benevolent, but uncompromisingly authoritarian procedures.

They took them along to church and sent them to Sunday School. They gave them creeds and catechisms to learn by heart. They taught them the biblical narratives and assured them that these stories carried the Word of God. They made them sing hymns and say prayers. It was realized that children would not understand much of all this, but it seemed to work out all right because the children stayed in the church, and grew up in due course as 'practising Christians', when they came to understand what they had uncomprehendingly received. But the secret of the old time success lay not in the teaching, but in the continuing community. Jones Minor's faith was not the faith of the Church: it was faith in the Church, a trust in the persons who guided him and loved him. And because he grew up to adult life in the company of these same persons whom he trusted, he arrived one day at conviction of his own. He began to enjoy what the Gestalt psychologists call the Aha! experience. Aha! he said, when he came up against suffering and responsibility and demands on his power to love and to give, Aha! so that's what they were talking about.

When that curious episode occurred, in 1944, and a secular State in which only one in ten went to church, asked the Church to undertake the religious education of all its children, the Church, understandably enough, went into action with its own well-tried methods. It was forbidden to make all children go to church, or even to recommend that they should, but it tried to turn all schools into churches, with worship every day and Bible study once or twice a week, and to maintain the school itself as a 'Christian community'. The answer the Church gave to the challenge of the Act was to say, Yes, we can bring up your children to religion by wrapping them in the life of the Church.

The fatal flaw in this theory was that boys and girls left this child-shaped church precisely at the moment of decision, and plunged into a world where only adult-shaped institutions had any appeal. Most of these youngsters had no experience at first

D

hand of an adult-shaped church. There was no personal link for them with people they trusted, to keep them within call to the moment of insight. The people they did trust never went near a church, and regarded it with a good-natured contempt as a sort of hobby-club for those who had never grown up, from within which, from time to time, there could be heard growling condemnation of drink or Sunday games or sex, or plaintive appeals for money to restore crumbling buildings. In such a situation, it is not unnatural that boys and girls in the process of becoming adults should turn their backs on the kid's stuff they had grown out of: Bible and prayer, hymn-singing, incomprehensible beliefs—the whole child-shaped system to which they had been exposed.

The hard facts of this situation are now well-enough known. An investigation[1] I have just completed into a number of schools where the religious education is thought to be particularly successful bears out the impressions we have been deriving from many sources. At the age of twelve slightly more than half the pupils claim to go to church 'regularly' or 'usually'. After three years of this 'successful' religious education, three-quarters have given up the habit of churchgoing; four-fifths have given up prayer; nine-tenths do not read their Bible at home. Three years later, as we know from other sources, nine-tenths will have finished with churchgoing, and we may make our own guess about the number of the faithful remnant who continue to pray or read the Bible for themselves. The main outlines of the situation are clear: that in the years before and after leaving school, our young people are registering with their feet a massive vote of no confidence in the Church.

It is against this background that we begin, for the first time, to ask strictly educational questions about our religious instruction. These hard facts make it plain that religious education comes to an end, for nine-tenths of our pupils, when

[1] *New Ground in Christian Education*, S.C.M. Press, 1965.

they leave school. Then what have they learnt, we ask, *before* they leave? Granted that the consummation of religious education, in full, active commitment to the Christian community, has not been achieved, is it not possible that they have learnt *something* from it all—a vision of life, a hunger and thirst after righteousness, something of a faith to live by, a sense of ultimate destiny to anchor them when the storms lash the waters about their little ship? 'Dear God, be good to me,' the Breton fishermen used to pray, 'for the sea is so large and my boat is so small.' Have our youngsters, as they push their craft eagerly down the sands to meet the waves, learnt just that degree of hope and courage and trust?

It is obvious that we are here dealing with something much less tangible, less open to measurement or demonstration than when we count the heads at church. The depths of our being lie beyond the reach of our slide-rule : the question is, in the end, unanswerable. To the tough-minded philosophers who say, Just what sort of evidence would you bring in answer to it, we are forced to reply, Yes, it *is* a pseudo-question. But we need not, perhaps, despair completely. We may perhaps be a little tough-minded ourselves, and though the final question eludes us, we may ask a number of preliminary questions to which answers may be found.

First, we can ask, How well do they know their Bibles, after ten years' acquaintance with it? The Agreed Syllabuses are agreed that Christian education, though more than Bible-knowledge, is to be conducted by means of Bible-knowledge. 'The Old Testament,' says Cambridgeshire, 'is more than the history of a chosen people; it is also a record of the development of ideas concerning Man and God, the relationship between them, and how man should live and behave. Using the historical background as a canvas, it will be possible in the later part of the course to trace in outline the development of these religious ideas through the Old Testament up to their culmination in the life and teaching of Jesus Christ.' 'The historical background as a canvas'—this is obviously meant to be the first, though not the last, part of the process. Then here is a question we can ask. How are we getting on with *this*? How well painted is the canvas? Have our boys and girls really mastered the chronology of the Bible, as a tool for digging in spiritual ground?

A group of teachers in Sheffield, working with their University Institute of Education, set out to answer this question by means of a fairly simple, factual test of religious knowledge, applied to 1,233 boys and girls of fourteen.[1] The inescapable conclusion emerged that the historical canvas was virtually blank. A few stray 'facts' were being retained—the meaning of Christmas Day, a few parables and miracles—but a grasp of historical sequence was totally lacking. In my recent survey of 'successful' schools, I applied the same test to 3,000 pupils from different parts of the country, to see if its depressing findings would be obtained elsewhere. They were, with an exactitude of correspondence that establishes, for the relatively simple test, a high degree of validity. We must face the fact that after ten years of religious education our boys and girls, launching their little boats, have no effective grasp of the development of the Bible story, or of the meaning of any but the most obvious events. Three-quarters of them do not know what Whitsuntide is about; less than 10 percent can arrange five Old Testament events in order; less than a quarter can recall the names of two prophetic writers; less than a quarter can recognize such descriptions as 'a great Israelite law-giver', 'said to have written many of the Psalms', 'a famous letter-writer of the New Testament'.

There can be argument over the importance we should attach to any single item here; but there can be no argument about the general proposition that boys and girls who cannot recall Moses, David, two prophets, St Paul or Pentecost are not masters of the historical background of the Bible to a degree that permits them to 'trace the development of the religious

[1] University of Sheffield Institute of Education, *Religion in Secondary Schools*, Nelson, 1961.

ideas through the Old Testament up to their culmination in the life and teaching of Jesus Christ'. If we set out to teach them the idea of revolution against a historical canvas of the eighteenth and nineteenth centuries, and our pupils could not recognize Rousseau or Robespierre or Napoleon or Wellington or say what Bastille Day was about, we should hazard the guess that they were not masters of the concept of revolution. The great hope behind the Agreed Syllabuses, that we should make the English people again, as they claimed to be during the Puritan revolution, a people of a Book, has been completely dashed. We cannot delude ourselves with the thought that our boys and girls, as they move so confidently away from church, are taking the Bible with them on a twentieth-century Pilgrim's Progress. By fifteen they have stopped reading it; and have virtually forgotten that they ever read it.

But at this point, another question arises, to the answering of which convincing evidence can be brought to bear. This is Ronald Goldman's question,[1] which runs: If the total narrative of the Bible, and the view of human life and man's developing understanding of God is not grasped, then what have our children understood of the parts as they went along? May it not be that though the canvas lacks the precise detail of a Dutch painting, it may nevertheless carry a vision of the numinous, like the French impressionists? May it not be that though the workings of God in history are beyond our pupils powers to see, the hand of God may have been seen in a few unrelated events?

I cannot do justice to Goldman's sophisticated and exacting research in these few moments, but his general argument is easily stated. He exposed a number of children, you will remember, to the stories of the Burning Bush, the Crossing of the Red Sea, and the Temptation to turn stones into bread; and asked them questions on their understanding of the episodes. Up to a mental age of seven or eight they responded with what

[1] *Religious Thinking from Childhood to Adolescence*, Routledge and Kegan Paul, 1964.

Goldman, following Piaget, describes as 'preoperational intuitive thought'—jumping to conclusions, seizing on one random element after another, mostly in terms of magic. Then until thirteen or fourteen they made attempts at coherent explanation, but explanation always in terms of the concrete situation, literally accepted, with no breakthrough to generalization or abstraction. Only after thirteen did they show themselves capable of formal, abstract operational thinking—which is the kind of thinking we do when we speak meaningfully about God.

Let me illustrate from the comments on the crossing of the Red Sea. 'How do you explain the dividing of the waters of the Red Sea?' produced, at the first stage, either irrelevance or magic.

> 'The man ran past the blue sea and the white sea. The blue sea went on one side and the white sea the other side.' When asked how the sea was divided, this aspect was dropped and the child replies 'Moses done it.' Similar to this is the child who centres upon the magical act, and this alone provides him with a satisfactory answer, 'God did it. He would magic it.' ... 'It was a miracle. God told Moses to put his hand out. It was magic.'

At the next stage, children attempted to *think*, to produce a theory, but it was a specific, concrete theory, unrelated to a general view of life and the way it works.

> 'God stretches his spirit over the water and that divides it.' 'God's palms (of his hands) were pushing them apart. You couldn't see them because they were invisible. When the Israelites were through he took his hands away and the waters flooded back.'
>
> 'God told the sea to part.' Has the sea got ears so it can hear? 'No.' Is it alive so it hears God? 'Oh yes, it can go one way or go another way. 'How do we know a thing is alive? 'Because it moves.'

By thirteen or fourteen an attempt is made to reconcile this event with natural law learnt in other areas of the curriculum.

'It's been proved that at a special time the sea does part. It gets very shallow.' How do you mean? 'At a special time of the year, only once a year.' Did God do it? 'No, they just got there at the right time. God had nothing to do with the sea, but he knew about it and got them there at the right time.'

Another attempt is more learned:

'All things are possible with God ...' How would God do it? 'He might take away the kinetic energy of the molecules on the surface of the water and a sheet of ice would form to keep the waters back.'

Now this still will not do: it is not the end of the matter. It is, however, the beginning, the first achievement of the kind of thinking that, when it is pursued, demands the concept of 'God'.

Goldman's case, in brief, is that before a mental age of thirteen or fourteen, children lack the necessary intellectual apparatus to think about 'God' at all. If we try to talk about God to them, they will seize on some irrelevant item in our discourse and turn it into the concrete imagery of their own mental world. The way this works with the 'God concept' is to be seen in the views of fourteen-year-olds assembled in *Teenage Religion*.[1] It is roughly true to say that at the chronological age of fourteen and a half two-thirds will have attained a mental age of fourteen, one-third will not. Predictably, then, a third of the pupils were still thinking about God in anthropomorphic terms: 'a person with three heads', 'an old man with longish white hair and nice clean-shaven face, with blue eyes like my grandfather's', 'an old man with long hair and a beard, wearing white robes, with a nice calm face and that', 'a old wise face, the most lovest eyes twincling a little and laughing

[1] S.C.M. Press, 1961.

at our little arrers'. The other two-thirds were struggling through to more formal, 'operational' categories:

> 'I imagine him as a sought of Ghost or spirit.'
>
> 'Sometimes I imagine him as a great shining light.'
>
> 'I can't imagine what God looks like, because he is a spirit and no one has ever seen him.'
>
> 'God or Jehovah is a spirit and no man has seen him but in the scriptures it says that all the jewels in the world would not near match his glory.'

This last, we might think, is beginning to arrive at a mature concept, but it is a rare instance. The majority of those who escape from childish concepts are really giving up the struggle.

> 'I haven't imagined him at all. All I know is that there must be someone, but who I don't know.'
>
> 'I don't think many people think about him at all.'

One or two echo the argument about 'God in the gaps':

> 'I think God is an imageanry thing in men's minds for them to fall back on when they come across something they dont understand, or when they are beaten by something.'

Others operate on the theological level of a Russian astronaut:

> 'I do not believe there is a God. Where could he be: he could not be in space, for all we know space goes on and on.'

Still others echo Freud: God is a man-made illusion.

> 'God could be the result of pagan ceremonys many millions of years ago, when the people of that time had great faith in their prayers, and created him to receive them.'
>
> 'I dont think there is anyone up there, it is just what we have been made to believe.'

Now all this would be splendid stuff if it were the *beginning* of religious thinking: the issues are all here—the problem of imagery, the problem of a naturalist world-view, the psychology of projection, the problem of transcendence and immanence. But this is not the beginning: for 90 percent it is the end, for they go to a world in which they will never hear the name of God again except as an oath. And, let us face it, it is the end for some of the 10 percent as well, who go to listen to a clergyman operating with the 'God concepts' of a ten-year-old.

The educational significance of *Honest to God*, if I may be permitted a glance at that controversy, is not so much in what it says as in what it asks. Well, then, teacher, it asks, What do you *mean* when you speak of 'God'? There is no harm in not liking what John Robinson says *he* means, or in feeling that 'depth of existence' or 'ground of being' are inadequate metaphors. Of course they are. But there is great harm if we just go red and gobble, and yammer, 'When I say God I mean God.' We must, if we are to be honest to children, come off our supernaturally high horse and speak of the human experiences that bring us to the point of disclosure where we see the 'shining light', the glory 'that all the jewels in the world would not near match'.

What we are doing to our children, with all our metaphysical machinery, is confusing them. I sampled their beliefs with some simple propositions about the Creation, about Jesus, and about suffering—the propositions representing a broad division into 'Christian orthodox', 'Christian agnostic', 'atheist agnostic' and 'atheist orthodox' points of view. Beliefs about the Creation divided equally on both sides of the central line: the majority were either 'Christian agnostic' or tentatively atheist. Beliefs about Jesus and God's purpose in suffering were almost entirely Christian, heavily biassed towards the orthodox. So we are left with the oddity that Jesus was the Son of the Creator, three-quarters believe that Jesus was the Son of the Creator. Over a third of the total believe in the divinity of Christ but do not believe in divinity. These are findings matched by the Mass Observation study of some years ago.

when 'Puzzled People' were found praying to a God they claimed not to believe in. We can make what we like of the implications, but one thing is certain: we have not trained our pupils in rigorous theological thinking.

And now I have one more note of gloom to strike before I try to sound a note of hope. The gloom concerns school assembly, that collective act of corporate worship compulsory on all schools and all pupils except those removed at the request of parents. The picture here is not all gloomy: there is a good deal of evidence that some children enjoy it and approve of it: 'It helps you to start the day off good,' said a third-form girl. And the Newsom Committee was entitled to take this sort of evidence seriously. But there is evidence on the other side. Consider this little speech, made in an earnest discussion in a modern school.

> Well you go in and get the old hymn books and you wait and the headmaster goes on about something and you dont understand it, with all them thees and thous and go verily. You have to stand up like that. It's murder for quarter of an hour. Teachers dont even 'ave to shut up. They're talking all the time. Then if you talk you're sent for and given the stick. It's using violence in God's name. They should know half of us dont take no notice of it. It's stupid really if you fink it out. You go in there to worship God and then some-one comes in and goes on about yer 'air and yer bell-bottomed jeans or somefink—what's it matter?

They complain about overcrowding:

> We are too squashed up and it is hard to concentrate with someone's foot in your back.

They complain about sitting on the floor, and about popping up and down 'like yoyos':

> It's more like a P.E. lesson, up and down, up and down.

They complain about monotony:

It would be helpful if different children read the Bible each morning and that Mr B. did not read such babish stories.

I get fed up with the same old readings.

Many just sing the hymns and say the prayers like someone in a trance—they mean nothing. It's always hymn, prayer, reading and another prayer—let's have a bit more variety now and again.

We should agree that some assemblies will be better than others; that the physical conditions, the forms used, the sincerity of those taking part, will all vary; and I have no statistics here, to indicate the significance of the protest. But protest there is, and in many schools it comes from the more serious pupils, who feel themselves to be under duress, compelled to take part in an act which they do not feel able to perform. 'Nobody has a right to make us pray,' said one girl to her headmistress. 'But I don't,' she replied, 'I don't *make* you pray.' 'But you try to, Miss, you say Let us pray.'

There is a certain oddity in all this, is there not, that a secular country should use the mighty machinery of an act of parliament to compel agnostic headmasters (for Christian headmasters need no compulsion) to conduct Christian worship for the children of unbelievers, who themselves lack the mental apparatus to grasp the concept of God; and to leave them bored, cynical and angry. I am not sure what the answer is, but I am sure that the whole discussion of the subject is shot through with humbug, and that daily in a thousand schools the lovely springs of the Christian experience are being muddied by earthbound men.

If we look back at the story thus far, we are left with a dismal picture of failure. We try for ten years to teach the 'facts' of the Bible, and we fail. We encourage our pupils to read it for themselves, and they refuse. We try to convey, through the Biblical narratives, the development of the idea of God, and we fail. We gather our pupils together for a total of 2,000 daily acts of worship, and we leave the vast majority indifferent, hostile, or bitterly resentful. Within the year, they will have cut themselves off entirely from Bible, Christian imagery and Christian practice, and will take nothing with them except muddled memories of life in a child-sized church.

But what of the ray of hope I promised? To explain this I must go back to a number of personal impressions, in themselves no more than straws in a wind. The first concerns my own students, some of whom say to me, 'Look, I can't do with your Christian metaphysics. It is all non-sense. But I'm as concerned as you are to help adolescents through their troubles, to find a reason for living, a faith, if you like, to live by. But it must be a faith based on persons and personal relationships, not on a God "up there".' The second set of impressions came to me as I walked about secondary schools with my tape-recorder trying to feel and hear what made for 'success' in religious education. At first, it seemed there was not a great deal to hear: a little exciting dramatic work in which I found the authentic note of Christian experience; a little honest discussion, in which I heard the beginnings of the analysis of Christian experience; but for the most part I found myself concurring with the view quoted in *Teenage Religion* that 'Scripture lessons are totally boring. One is inclined to sit back and let the teacher do the work.' But after a time I began to hear things that were not on the surface, things that my tape-recorder would miss. I heard tones of voice, I saw expressions on faces, I sensed a sort of urgency of concern. These men and women, talking so much and so incomprehensibly, looked and sounded as if they *cared*, cared not only for the subject they taught but the children they taught it to, cared not only that they should 'learn the subject' but should find through it re-assurance and hope and vision. And I watched the children's eyes and faces and listened to the tones of their voices—when they were allowed to talk at all—and I had the hunch that they knew about this concern, that they felt themselves to be cared for and valued. They were often bored; but then, many of these entwined couples that pass us in the street look bored too; and they would be the first to tell us that being bored-in-love is better than being just bored.

So far, my hunches, my straws in the wind, suggesting that despite our conceptual failure, our failure, if you like to teach theology, we are nevertheless conveying, in some schools, an experience of Christian love that is educative at a deep level. And let us give honour here to the Agreed Syllabuses, who warned us that this might happen. Cambridgeshire said, way back in 1924,

> If Christianity is a way of life, it cannot be imparted by intellectual formulations in the way that mathematics can be : it can be learnt only from experience, not from discourse. 'By love may He be gotten and holden, but by thought never.'

This hunch of mine cannot be put to the test, but there are two tests I applied that begin to bear on it. The first consisted of three simple attitude scales concerned with obedience to parents, kindness to animals, and the colour problem. The attitudes ranged from tough-minded to tender-minded; and were designed to group young people into four broad categories of response. Were they, I was asking, as tough-minded about parents, animals and coloured people as they were about the Bible and going to church? They emerged triumphantly on the tender-minded side, declaring themselves, with a unanimity they match in no other area, more compassionate and less 'realistic', if you like, than we are. The results bear out a *New Society* survey of similar attitudes a couple of years ago, in which the teenage years and the twenties affirmed themselves as the period of compassion and hope, to be followed by the increasing realism and compromise that produce, in due time, the people you and I are.

There is here an assertion of persons, the voice of concern, a declaration of caring, that seems to me evidence of a response to persons, and concern and caring. I am not claiming this as a triumph for religious education in the classroom alone. It is 'in the culture' that amalgam of hope and fear, magnanimity and greed, love and selfishness that we breathe as we grow and live and work and play. But I stick at the fact that our youngsters are here away out ahead of us, and I believe that the school, with its own form of tender-mindedness, is supporting them and pushing them on.

The other test I applied was a semantic differential test centred on the Christian image. What ideas do you have in your mind, I asked, when you read the words 'a real Christian'? They were then offered pairs of adjectives to select from: easy ones like 'good' and 'bad', 'forgiving and unforgiving', 'generous' and 'mean'; more loaded ones like 'sincere' and 'hypocritical', 'sociable' and 'unsociable', 'old-fashioned' and 'modern'; and some irrelevancies, to catch them out: 'easy-going' and 'strict', 'conventional' and 'unconventional', 'rich' and 'poor'. Their responses were wholly accurate. They declared the 'real Christian' to be good, generous, sociable and forgiving, strong-willed, confident, reliable and sincere. The irrelevancies they dismissed as irrelevant, declaring the real Christian to be neither old-fashioned nor modern, conventional nor unconventional, rich or poor, easy-going or strict.

Now here again I do not want to make larger claims than the test will justify. There are many tough-minded, cautionary comments we could make to whittle down its meaning: that 'Christian' is a halo word in our culture, as 'democratic' is in America; that these are merely humane virtues, the mark of any good man—and so we could continue. Yet there is surely something of hope here: when a crowd of youngsters who have rejected the Bible, rejected the Church, declared themselves bored by scripture lessons and angry about school prayers, when such a crowd give a nearly unanimous and entirely favourable response to the Christian image of personality, this surely means something.

There is another sign of encouragement. In commenting on the *Teenage Religion* findings I drew attention to the liveliness and amplitude of the children's discussions and writings:

Any teacher who has tried to provoke a discussion in English or history will perceive that the discussions 'went' with a genuine life and vigour. Any teacher who has collected up compositions on Spring or Patriotism or A Railway Station will recognize that the comments on our papers come from people who have something to say.... Furthermore, they have been interested for some time. The questions we posed were, after all, extensive in their range: the existence and nature of God, the divinity of Christ, eternity, sacrifice, ethics, educational method. These are not issues to which we should expect much prior attention from the gang of school-boys whom we see tumbling off the school bus. Yet the confidence and eagerness with which they attack our questions, the rarity of the confession, 'I have not thought much about this,' the air, so frequently noticeable, of 'I have an answer to that one,' the frequency of those answers that try to find a reason why other people believe differently—all this conveys an impression that thought has been going on and minds have been at work.

That their minds *are* at work—or at least eager to get to work—is borne out by the last piece of evidence I want to produce: the virtual unanimity of the desire to replace talk and chalk by discussion.

I would like to see more discussing than just writing on the board and copying it down blindly.

I think it would be better if we didn't do so much writing but discussed the bible more often I would be more likely be able to understand it better then as I think it is hard to understand.

And, my favourite among them all,

I like a scripture lesson when you are at ease with the teacher, when you argue and have it out with the teacher about certain points. I like to have debates about unexplainable things to get nearer to the truth!

It is all there, is it not? 'Unexplainable things', 'argue and have it out', 'at ease with the teacher', 'get nearer to the truth'. Here we have the outline of what our young people will respond to, if only we can meet them: the recognition on our part that in religious education we deal with uncertainties, with mystery that we cannot tie down in formulae; the recognition that our youngsters have been in the world for a dozen years or more, and have things they need to say and ask and defend, as they explore their own experience and make their own search; the recognition that they need to be at ease with us and we with them, open to each other in candour and sincerity; and the recognition—rather hard to come by as we look at the row of apathetic faces—that they really want, beneath it all, to 'get nearer to the truth'.

I believe that the pains these young things go through as they come of age will be met when we can lay them open to the knowledge that we too are coming of age, and find it painful; when we can confess that we are not ultimately certain of our ground, yet that we know we must stand on it, stand as if we were certain, stand certainly; when we can open the dialogue, true dialogue, I-thou and thou-I; when we can learn to trust them to be what they are, young slaves escaping from their slavery—and even in these child-centred days, infancy is still slavery; escaping across the Red Sea of their self-assertion, where we cannot follow them, into a waste land where they must go to and fro at the bidding of their own leaders, and see the desert horizons under the scorching sun, and meet their own moral imperative and try to follow it, and fail, and judge themselves, and now fight their enemies and now give way to them, and become affluent and be attracted to strange gods and strange ways. This is what lies before them, and we are powerless to lead them into the promised land of self-discovery. Themselves alone can find the ground of their being. But they have powers to help them. They have a kind of hope, a hope that they will leave the world better than they found it, and will find happiness in their task. They have a kind of loving, not perhaps as regulated or as accepting as ours was, but for all that there is love in it. And they have a kind of faith, a faith in persons. My young people, too, claimed a faith in a Person—how deep or informed I do not know; but they claimed it.

Be that as it may, they have the root of two parts of the great triad of the Christian experience. It may be that they will find a new shape to their faith: it may be that we cannot give them the faith of our fathers, yet that they will find a faith for their children in which the humaneness of the humanist, the humility that dares to be agnostic, the morality that springs from compassion rather than the rule book, the spontaneity and eagerness and irreverence and laughter of our boys and girls may yet fuse into a religion that is truly personal, because personally discovered. After all, this is what happened to the Hebrews, who were slaves and free and then lost and exiled and at odds with themselves, and lost the faith of their fathers under the new impulse of a faith in a Person. May it be that *this* is what is going to happen again?

E

CHAPTER IV

RELIGIOUS EDUCATION IN THE SECONDARY SCHOOL
(b) *Defining a Policy*

DAVID AYERST

The kind of policy I am going to talk to you about is largely concerned with what we might call the logistics of religious instruction—the conditions which are necessary if we are to make anything like a success of the job we have to do. It is my belief, based on a good many years' experience of seeing what is going on, (and of seeing what is not going on) that one reason why the results of the last twenty years work are so much less than we might have hoped is simply that we have not begun to provide the necessary conditions for success. Where those conditions exist there is in my view no reason to despair.

Forgive me if in describing what exists, I repeat what many of you know only too well. It is well to get the record straight. I start with the modern school because that is still the school to which something like two-thirds of our boys and girls go. Something like two-thirds of these schools provide two periods a week for religious education just as they provide two periods a week for history and geography and five or six periods a week for mathematics. I doubt if very much new thought has gone into thinking out time-table allocations. It is just how things are. This holds true for the first three years of the Secondary course. In the fourth year there is a tendency to reduce the time given to the subject, though over half the schools still stick to two periods for everybody. This process is carried further with the fifth form, where one exists. Leaving examination sets out of account, about a quarter of the schools seem to stick to two periods a week in the fifth year and another quarter to assume that the compulsory clauses of the 1944 Act no longer apply and to do without. Most of the remainder settle for a single period.

It is then, at the top end of the modern school that there has been some new thinking about time-table allocations; and this has been largely the result of the pressure on the total teaching time available for substantially increased allowances for those subjects which are going to be externally examined. Other subjects are cut or cut out. Religious education, as I have said, is usually in the former category, sometimes in the latter. Sometimes, but not always, it is in the favoured list of subjects which get more time for those who opt to take an external examination in it. About two-fifths of modern schools with fifth forms are in this category. It is distinctly more common in girls' schools than in boys' or mixed schools.

In all this, the modern school is getting more like the grammar school. And this is quite right when one remembers how very rough and ready the division between pupils of grammar school calibre and others is at the point of selection. In grammar schools, a single religious education period for all forms applies to two-thirds of the forms in the second year of the course, and to three-quarters or more for the remainder of it. Only in the first year do the majority of forms get two periods, and even so, it is only a bare majority. In the second year, the proportion with two periods is down to a quarter and thereafter it steadily dwindles. Here I think we should note two things. The slimming process starts earlier in the grammar school than in the modern. This is not, in my view, because grammar school heads are more averse to religious education than modern school heads, but because the whole process of specialization starts earlier. It is from the third year on, sometimes even from the second, that what Crowther called the policy of pre-specialization starts in grammar schools. In modern schools, it does not start until the third, or more often the fourth year. At this point, whichever it is, the policy of

cut or cut out inevitably begins to operate, given the super-
stitious English belief that all GCE subjects should be equivalent
in some mysterious way, which in practice seems to mean that
they should have approximately the same amount of teaching
time in and about the examination year. I simplify here a little,
but I think the general principle is clear. In grammar schools
the treatment applied to religious education is 'cut'; to history
or geography it is more often 'cut out'—they commonly become alternatives. Both methods are unsatisfactory. I do not
think that the friends of history, geography or religious education will have any chance of getting a solution which will be
satisfactory from their point of view unless they can get the
problem of the curriculum tackled as a whole, and get something done about pre-specialization and the equivalence of
GCE, and, I expect, of CSE subjects. It is a mistake to think of
religious education as a solitary victim. I could wish that in
considering the ineffectiveness of religious education more
attention were paid to the research done at Leeds a good many
years ago now by Mr J. W. Packer which showed that the
waters of Lethe wash out historical knowledge almost as
thoroughly as religious.[1]

The position in the comprehensive schools resembles closely
that in the grammar schools. It is natural that it should, for
those who would otherwise be in grammar schools or in the
external examination streams of modern schools. But there is
nothing in the nature of the case to suggest that this should
apply to all pupils in comprehensive schools or indeed to more
than a bare majority. In fact, it commonly applies to all, irres-
pective of ability.

So much then for how much teaching gets done. The next
question is, 'Who does it?' The myth of religious education
given by an army of unbelieving conscripts dies hard. It cir-
culates, and oddly enough it seems to be received with equal

[1] J. W. Packer: Report presented to University of Leeds Institute of
Education 1952. 'Enquiry into the amount of religious learning and
history possessed by pupils of sixteen and eighteen'.

glee, in clerical meetings and secularist assemblies. But myth it is as far as the county secondary schools today are concerned. As nearly as I can estimate the proportion of teachers giving religious education in all county secondary schools is only about one in seven; there is not a great deal of variation between boys', girls' and mixed schools; but there are marked differences between modern, selective and comprehensive schools. The proportion varies between these groups from about a fifth in modern schools (it was well over a third ten years ago) to about 5 percent in comprehensive schools. Within ten years the proportion of modern schools where virtually every form master takes his own form for religious education has dropped from something approaching a third to 2 percent or thereabouts. Five years ago it was nearly a fifth. Clearly, there should be no difficulty in the way of any secondary teacher taking advantage of the conscience clause, a fact which ought to be quite as re-assuring to the Christian as to the atheist.

It is I think fair to say that the great majority of those who do give religious education in secondary schools do so because they want to, or because they think they ought to. This is good; but how well qualified are they for the job? Some have all the knowledge they need of the subject matter. Others find themselves out of their depth when their pupils begin to probe. At least four-fifths have no specialist qualification, and this proportion by any standard is too high. Only about one in eight have a university degree or diploma or have had full-time training on one of the Department's supplementary courses. Some are ministers of religion, and some of them have forgotten in the pulpit the art of listening, which is an essential part of teaching. It is a little difficult to believe that those responsible for the supply and training of teachers have given this subject quite the attention that it needs. It looks as if the schools with their rapid swing away from the class teacher system have been more on their toes than the authorities at the Town Hall and the Centre. Is it not a pity that the liberating effect of the 1944 Act, which made it possible for the first time for specialists to be employed in the general run of schools, was not followed first by an enquiry made without pre-conceived ideas to discover what being a religious education specialist ought to involve, and then by a determined campaign to see that they were forthcoming and were employed? It is late, but not too late. Both steps are necessary. We need to give much more attention than we have yet done to the kind of job a religious education specialist has to do and to the kind of preparation that this involves. This is quite as important as taking steps to increase the supply. Unless it is done, we might easily find ourselves landed with the wrong sort. And this would be disaster.

How do we use the teachers we have? If we were to devise a scale of subjects arranged in the order in which pupils and teachers needed to have real personal knowledge of one another, religious education would almost certainly come nearly at the top of the list, and probably right at the top. But it is in practice a subject in which there is less possibility of close personal knowledge than in almost any other. This is certainly true in selective and comprehensive schools. Let us do a little arithmetic. A secondary school teacher probably teaches thirty periods a week. If his subject is mathematics or a foreign language he is unlikely to take more than six forms or sets a week; and, if this is so, he will meet about 180 boys and girls each week. If he teaches history or geography and takes one 'O' level set and no sixth form advanced work, his probable score will be 420 different pupils each week. It will be about the same if he is a religious education specialist in a school which devotes two periods a week to the subject. If in addition to 'O' level work there is some 'A' level the number of different faces each week might well be reduced to 360, but this is still more than most of us would feel that we can know in any real personal sense. For schools with a single weekly period for religious education, these figures can roughly be doubled. These very rough calculations are based on the assumption that religious education specialists teach religious education and nothing else. What is the likelihood of that? On the basis of one period a week per form, a school would need to be about 900 strong to justify one specialist without any examination work. About 250 secondary schools fall into this category. About half the total number of secondary schools in the country would justify an exclusive religious education specialist on the basis of a flat two periods a week. And the number and proportion of big secondary schools is growing. In 1953 about 30 percent of secondary schools had 400 or more pupils, and there were only forty-six schools with more than 800 pupils. In 1963, the corresponding figures were 58 percent and 392 (7 percent). The process continues. It seems probable that where teachers with good qualifications are in short supply the bigger schools will tend to get them, and those schools which have specialists are likely to spread them as widely as possible across the time-table. This may very well not be in the teacher's interest, or the pupil's, but it is a human weakness to like to teach one's own subject, and I suspect that the specialists are sometimes consenting parties to the impossible task they are often asked to do. Moreover, if they do stick out for being allowed to teach some other subject as well, there is often no guarantee that this will be arranged in such a way as to reduce the total number of faces they see each week. They may well find themselves teaching a form history or civics instead of religious education and not as well as religious education.

In a large secondary school, I personally should like to see a religious education team of one or two specialists whose main job lies in that and who 'majored', to use a useful Americanism, in the theological field. I should want them to be supported by a few colleagues whose main concern is with some other subject. I should want the religious education specialists to spend a little of their time teaching some other subject, both for their own relief and in order to give them the opportunity of seeing some of their pupils a little more frequently than the scanty religious education allocation allows. For this reason, their supporting subject is better if it is one which has a small time allocation itself—if it is history, a good choice, then five or six periods a week say, bring them into contact with ninety pupils whereas, if it were French, it would only give them thirty pupils a week. For their sake, this supporting role should be with forms at about the lowest level in the school at which they take religious education, because once you have got to know a boy or girl, you go on knowing him and he, you.

So much for theory. How does it work out in practice? The best estimate I can make is that about one teacher in six of those who give religious education teach it to ten or more forms each week, i.e. to probably more than 300 different boys and girls. Six percent teach fifteen or more forms and 2 percent twenty or more forms. The largest number of forms taught each week by the same teacher in the group of schools from which I am now generalizing was twenty-seven, or roughly 800 pupils. I do not want to press these figures too far, but they are in line with my general experience and I do not think they are far out. It seems clear, too, that it is the best qualified teachers who carry the most dispersed load. In the group of schools to which I have referred teachers with full theological qualifications formed only 7 percent of the total number of religious education teachers, but they taught 17 percent of the forms.

It would seem pretty clear that a good deal of careful enquiry ought to be made—and not only in the interest of religious education—into the optimum teaching load in terms of pupils per teacher per week. Even without this enquiry, I think it can be said that, in religious education, we are obviously not using our best qualified teachers to best advantage; and that nobody need be surprised if the results of enquiries into pupils' attainments in religious education prove disappointing. It would be a miracle if they did not. And as far as education is concerned, I would cheerfully adopt the title of Toland's famous work *Christianity not Mysterious*. There is no mystery about some at least of the reasons for the weakness of religious education.

There is one other measurable aspect of the staffing position for religious education which ought to be mentioned. There is reason to believe that the proportion of graduates to non-graduates in religious education is not very much above half the proportion of graduates to non-graduates in secondary school staffs as a whole. This is natural enough because most of the training college men and women giving religious education will at least have had some sort of a course in it at college, and some of them will have made a fairly substantial study. Among graduates, apart from those who are graduates in theology, there will usually be the diffidence born of ignorance, however much good-will there may be. They will tend to hold back if somebody who knows a little more is available. It may very well be that for a good many of the teaching posts in secondary schools, a good training college background may be preferable for the religious education specialist to a university one—I am not concerned to argue that here—but there is no doubt that its public esteem is less, and no doubt also that the proportion of secondary school teachers who are graduates is rising and will continue to rise. In 1953, it was 39 percent; in 1963, it was 51 percent. There is a real problem here of status and pay for the surviving non-graduates, which must be faced.

My subject is defined for me as secondary education; but I may perhaps be pardoned if I look for a moment over my shoulder from the bottom end of the secondary school to the very similar boys and girls of the top end of the junior school. The primary school is still very firmly committed to the class teacher system, though perhaps a dangerous kind of educational heresy is beginning to make itself heard, the equivalent in pedagogics to the South Bank in theology. There are obvious disadvantages in any automatic assumption that every teacher ought to give religious education—Christians find it just as objectionable as secularists. The conscience clause ought theoretically to provide a remedy, but it is obvious that in practice it does not. I do not see myself that it can be made to work in practice unless we can get away from the sacred cow conception of the class teacher system. It may be very nice for a teacher to teach her class everything; it is certainly very bad for many teachers to have a go each week at a class of ten-year-olds; many of us in the secondary schools think that too many teachers at present are concerned with first- and second-year forms. If we can tackle the problem empirically and agree on the one hand, that not all teachers are or can be omniscient even within the little universe of study of the junior school, and on the other, that no ten-year-old ought to have more than three or at the most, four teachers in one week, we could soon get rid from religious education of the awkward squad of uneasy conscripts who are only not conscientious objectors because they are anxious not to be difficult. But I do not think we shall do it by concentrating on the problem in religious education. It is more likely to come as a result of the introduction of French and real mathematics into primary schools. The first breach in the class-teacher system came with the recognition that some teachers were tone deaf and that this has implications for music teaching. The breach needs enlarging.

Let us humble camp followers of the linguists and mathematicians consider what difference that would make to the teacher position for religious education. I think a good many people would be surprised at the number of teachers who would like to take part. There might well be more, as far as I can judge, than could well be trained for it. Certainly I should not look forward to anything like a specialist system. I should want to lay down as a general rule that nobody should teach children between the ages of nine and thirteen religious education, who didn't teach the same children some other subject. Equally, I should want to make sure that nobody was engaged in religious education who (a) had not had a good deal of training for it—something much nearer to a training college main course than a basic course; and (b) who had not got a sufficient amount of it to do each week to justify her in earmarking a fair proportion of her time for preparation and for refresher courses for this subject. This might involve a careful study of appropriate subject links and of sensible time allocations, not necessarily on as restricted a basis as a week. From this one ought to be able to work out the number of teachers who ought to be trained. We have in the popular Junior-Secondary courses in training colleges a suitable vehicle which could easily carry this new load.

There are only two comments I want to make on syllabus at this stage, and one inference I want to draw from them. I believe that boys and girls of this age have a passion for acquiring facts—collecting, docketting, cataloguing; and also a love of heroic story. I would try to satisfy these tastes in two ways. By setting the scene of the world into which Jesus came as fully and significantly as possible; and by sketching in as many of the great stories from Christian, not Old Testament, history as I could. Because a sense of historical development comes late, too much Old Testament is apt to give highly distorted ideas of the nature of God. I should want to do this double task in as straightforward and exciting a way as I could manage, and I should want to banish moralizing from my lessons. I should think it sensible to arouse interest in church buildings, and synagogues too, and to explore why they are as they are in shape and use. But I should not want to proselytize. There must certainly be a conscience clause for parents; but I should want my teaching to be such that, even if none existed, there could be no legitimate complaint about my teaching.

I have said something, not very much but as much as there is time for, about teachers. May I say also that as another consequence of a modified class teacher system I see a great need for LEA's to provide first-class advisers? Perhaps, as an old HMI, you will allow me to say how warmly I welcomed the decision of the West Riding to appoint an adviser, of the care taken to find one; and how enheartened I have been by the consequences. And that goes for Norfolk too.

This brings me to the middle and upper levels of secondary schools as they are now organized. If the schools had not made their own preferences abundantly clear, I should have felt the need to argue for the provision of suitably-trained specialists. They have saved me the trouble. There is no doubt they are wanted. Where a demand exists, it is likely to get filled one way or another. And so it is with religious education, but I am not at all happy about the way it is being met at present; nor do I think the schools are. It seems to me that we ought to be able to rely on the universities to provide suitable people. The trouble is that it is very doubtful whether university courses in theology give the right background. The heavy linguistic demands they make are far from the needs of the schools. This in itself is not to condemn them. Universities are not vocational preparatory schools, and it would be wrong to expect everything in a degree course to be directly relevant to teaching needs. But there are, I feel, three reasons for dissatisfaction with the present system. First, the linguistic and textual needs are such as to make it impossible to carry far enough some of the studies that are really necessary. Some of these are available as options, but options tend to be peripheral to a course, while it is the frontier subjects, dealing with the relation of religion to other disciplines, which need to be pretty close to the centre of the religious education specialist's equipment today. The second reason for dissatisfaction is perhaps not directed against the universities direct as against the consequences of their linguistic demands, given the present organization of the schools. If one is to do well in a theological school one should be a reasonably good linguist at school; and, as schools are, that means that one would not have carried one's science very far. But to be innumerate is a serious handicap to understanding the modern world. If there is not to be an almost complete failure of communication between the religious education specialist and about half his sixth form pupils there may well be need for him to go through something like the first year at Keele before embarking on his theological studies. The third reason for dissatisfaction arises from the academic status of the theological courses in which linguistic studies play either no part or a minor one. Usually these courses are for a general degree and do not attract men and women of the calibre we need.

There is no doubt that in selective and comprehensive schools the principal religious education specialist needs to be a person of real ability. The exposition of Christianity today, its communication to the sceptical but ignorant, and participation in general contemporary intellectual discussion demands a subtlety of mind, a lively honesty in thought, and a power to understand what another person is saying however badly he says it and then to answer him in similar, but not misleading terms. These are rare gifts. We need the best. University courses do not seem, to an outsider like myself, designed to give us the best. Is it worth somebody's while to try to bring universities and schools together to work at the pattern of study which would best meet the intellectual needs of the schools of today?

I have left myself little time in which to deal with what the teachers ought to be doing in the middle and upper parts of secondary schools. I shall have to content myself with a brief mention of some of the things that seem to me important. Very high on the list I should put the introduction of some element of choice into the religious education programme. The Education Act safeguards the parent's conscience if he cares to avail himself of its protection—but very few except Roman Catholics do. It gives the seventeen- or eighteen-year-old boy or girl no such protection. But they have reached the age when nearly all would agree that their integrity deserves quite as much respect. If I read the signs aright, I think we should go far to enlist their support if it were possible to provide a range of options within the field of religious, moral and philosophical studies between which they would be free to choose. Wise tutoring would probably not find it difficult to secure a reasonable balance over a period of two or three years, breaking up the options into units of a term's duration. Such a programme would require great skill in time-tabling and could hardly be carried out in schools where only one teacher was willing and equipped to take part. There is no doubt from the survey of sixth form opinion which Mr Edwin Cox and his associates have been carrying out that sixth formers greatly value discussion periods. I have some doubt from conversations with training college students whether in retrospect they feel they were quite as good value for money as they thought at the time. 'We only discussed.' It seems to me that what the sixth formers really value is the escape from spoon-feeding and from the feeling that they are being 'got at'. They become dissatisfied when later on they discover that there is nothing to show in the end for all their talk. I believe a system of options, provided that such option had sufficient time given to it to make a real study possible, would meet both needs—the need to choose for oneself and the need to get something worth having from one's choice.

The way the educational world is going in sixth form organization suggests that what we may call the religious education options would have to be made available as part of the main general studies course. I should like to think that this was an unexamined field except in so far as the value became apparent in interviews. I wish I thought this was still a possibility, but the English so love all examinations except the eleven plus that I fear we must reconcile ourselves to general papers or general studies papers. If this is so, then it is surely essential that the whole field of religious, moral and philosophical studies should carry as much weight as politics and mathematics. This is not so now.

I move back one or two years to the stage when boys and girls are preparing for their 'O' levels or for CSE. Once again it is necessary to see how the contributions we have to make to their education can best be fitted into the general pattern of school work at this stage. I hope that we shall not be quiet about what we dislike about the general pattern, but for the time being it is something to which we have to conform. There seems to me to be little reason to doubt that the tyranny of old GCE priest will be reinforced, though I hope not written larger, by that of new CSE presbyter. The very great bulk of the pupils' time and almost the whole of their attention to school work at this stage will be concentrated on the subjects they will be offering for external examination. An unexamined subject is going to get scant justice if it is treated in the orthodox way. This then is the stage, rather than the sixth form, when we might most profitably use discussion group techniques—the more so as this is the period when personal and social ethical problems are often uppermost in the minds and lives of boys and girls. My own solution here would be to be severely practical, dealing with problems of their own choice without authoritative direction, and coupling work in the classroom with opportunities for social service ventures on an entirely and genuinely voluntary basis.

This, then, is one way in which we might provide general religious education for the last three or four years of secondary school life—discussion and problem solving in the years of 'O' level pressure; followed by philosophical and theological units in a general studies programme in the sixth form. But I should not want religious education to be regarded as a subject unsuitable for examination at either 'O' or 'A' level or the equivalent. I know that this is a matter on which schools differ greatly both in practice and in principle. In secondary schools as a whole just on half provide religious education courses for an external examination; about three-quarters of the comprehensive schools do so, and over half the selective. It seems to me right that in a school large enough to be able to offer a full range of subjects, the option should be left to the pupil. The opportunity should be there, and it should be there for all to take. The worst of all worlds is to provide an external examination course and confine it to weaker candidates. This happens far too often and could normally be avoided by determined skill in time-tabling. Recruitment of better candidates for religious education examination work in the sixth form might well be helped if the movement towards half subjects is successful, and if skill is shown in devising programmes which make a coherent whole with the main subjects most likely to be taken. A surgical operation on the existing 'A' level syllabus does not seem to me to be the most hopeful approach.

Between the 9-13 stage (perhaps we shall soon be able to remove the hyphen from the Junior-Secondary courses in training colleges) and the external examination years we are left with one or two years in which thorough straightforward teaching is possible and in which the principal attention could be given to Christ and the Gospels. But I don't want to appear to prescribe syllabus. In my view those who teach in a secondary school of any size should be led by a well-qualified specialist, and I should hope that those who draw up Agreed Syllabuses would recognize the changing situation and be willing to leave much more scope for free development to individual schools than has always been the case.

It may be that some will think what I have had to say unduly complacent. Nobody could fail to be aware of the pressure of the mass media exploiting the currently fashionable view that the only virtue of established things is to provide a target for cheap wit and a record of how stupid people have been. True enough, but moods change and so will this. There are, and I hope I have shown, sufficient obviously wrong things in the way we set about our task to encourage me to think that, if we have put them right by the time the public mood changes again, we ought to be able to do a very much better job than we have generally done up to now—as good a job, and it is a good one, as the best schools have already achieved. May I end with some words of Abraham Lincoln? 'It is said that an Eastern monarch once charged his wise men to invent him a sentence to be ever in view and which should be true and appropriate in all times and situations. They presented him the words "And this too shall pass away". How much it expresses! How chastening in the hour of pride! How consoling in the depths of affliction! "And this too shall pass away." And yet let us hope that it is not quite true. Let us hope rather that by the best cultivation of the physical world beneath and around us, and the intellectual and moral world within us, we shall secure an individual social, and political prosperity and happiness, whose course shall be onward and upward, and which, while the earth endures, shall not pass away.'

CHAPTER V

THE TRAINING OF TEACHERS OF RELIGIOUS EDUCATION

(a) Training Colleges and Colleges of Education

MARY PARNABY

The 1944 Education Act not only radically altered the position of religious instruction in schools, but also caused great changes to take place in training colleges. Before this, scripture or divinity or religious education was not a qualifying subject in the teacher's certificate, and colleges could only offer courses in it as an additional subject. In many colleges, particularly the voluntary ones, there were systematic courses given, and the Church training colleges entered their students for the Archbishop's Certificate in Religious Knowledge. In the LEA colleges the subject was usually taught by a member of staff whose main concern was with some other subject, the academic standard of the courses was not high, nor was much time spent on them; in some colleges a mass lecture once a week, given to a whole year at once for part of their course was as much as was offered.

The changes in the Education Act meant that much more provision for religious teaching must be made in the colleges if teachers were to be prepared to deal at all adequately with the kind of work outlined in the new agreed syllabuses, and it became necessary to appoint specialist staff. At first it was not easy to find the right people for these posts; the absence of very much teacher training in the field before this meant that there were few people who possessed both the necessary theological qualifications and training and experience in teaching. A considerable number of clergy of various denominations applied for posts as lecturers, and some have made a very valuable contribution indeed, but not all have the necessary teaching skill and experience. Over the years, however, the position has greatly improved, and most colleges now have fully qualified and experienced staff in this as in other departments.

For the factual information about the present position I am greatly indebted to the colleges themselves. I myself left England at the end of 1963,[1] and my experience was in any case limited to three colleges directly, and to a lesser extent, to others in the institute where I worked. Last autumn, therefore, I circularized all the general colleges, with the exception of the Roman Catholic ones in England and Wales asking for information, and I have received replies from ninety-one of them. The total number of students in these colleges is 37,607, and of these 3,540 (approximately 9 percent) are taking religious knowledge as the main subject in their course. Eighty-two of these colleges offer a main course in the subject, all except one also offer a basic or curriculum course taken by most, if not all students, and some offer a subsidiary course which falls somewhere between these two; some also offer an advanced main course for a few students. The lecturers in the colleges have been most generous in sending me not only direct answers to the questions asked, but also syllabuses of courses, and comments of a most helpful kind.

The three different courses have different aims and I propose briefly to consider each one in turn and finally to say a word about the supplementary course still offered in a few colleges for qualified teachers.

Firstly almost all colleges have a basic or curriculum course, taken in most cases by all students except those who have genuine conscientious objections. In some colleges special arrangements are made for small groups, e.g. for Roman Catholic students, who, on conscientious grounds, feel that they cannot attend the normal course. The basic course is

[1] On relinquishing appointment as vice-principal of the City of Leeds Training College.

designed not merely to give background information for teaching, though in many colleges this is its main aim, but also to help students to think about their own philosophy of life. Groups are inevitably very mixed in their background and attitude to the subject, ranging from those who are keenly interested and knowledgeable, who are eager to discuss and who want to teach scripture in schools, to those who not only have no interest, but who sometimes begin by being antagonistic to the idea of spending time on something which does not count towards their certificate (for basic courses are often not examined) and which they regard as being quite unimportant and irrelevant. This hostile attitude is not widespread, but it appears to be more common among men than among women; though some women students receive what they are given with a passivity which can be more exhausting for a lecturer than active hostility expressed in argument! The chief problem about the basic course is that in a very limited time (in some cases one period a week over two years, in others a more intensive course for a shorter period, and in a few, a course which does extend over three years) the lecturer is trying to do at least two things which are often incompatible. He is trying to give adequate biblical background for teaching purposes together with helping students in various ways to get some understanding of children's development and needs at various stages and the selection of material designed to meet those needs; and he is also trying to remove misconceptions and misunderstandings held by students; to enable them to think clearly and discuss problems of religion and ethics with understanding and tolerance. Too often students come up to college believing that to be Christian means subscribing unreservedly to large numbers of dogmas which intellectually they are unsure about or cannot accept, and some have rejected religion on these grounds. One lecturer writes: 'Fear and ignorance present blockages which take so much breaking down that training is over before much is accomplished by way of building up. Where they do not exist I think the students grow in maturity and in spiritual understanding as a consequence of what is put before them in these courses.' I said that the two aims of the course are sometimes incompatible; if one is to give even elementary biblical background to students many of whom have extremely little knowledge, it is necessary to spend a large proportion of the time lecturing, yet experience shows that formal lectures make little real impact and the material in them is not absorbed. In some colleges this problem has been partly solved by preparing assignments of work for individuals or groups of students, which involve reading background material and preparing teaching aids and notes. Similarly topics for discussions are drawn up and prepared beforehand. One college uses two entirely different basic syllabuses for different groups of students. The first is of the more conventional type, designed for those who are favourably disposed to the subject and want to be prepared to share in teaching it; it deals with the nature of religion, the aims of religious education, agreed syllabuses : their content and method of teaching, and with a study of Old and New Testaments and fundamental Christian doctrines. The alternative syllabus begins with an introductory survey of the western world, its ideologies and attitudes; it includes topics such as science and religion and scientific humanism; and it attempts to study philosophy as well as biblical criticism and the nature of biblical truth. But in practice it is wellnigh impossible to cover either of these syllabuses at all adequately in the very limited time available and at the same time give real opportunity for discussion. Nevertheless, although time is limited and only a small part of any previously prepared syllabus may be covered, although some students may remain passive throughout and gain little from the basic course, there is evidence that others have been stimulated and helped; those who already have some interest in and knowledge of the subject have developed a much greater understanding of the Bible and have been enabled to make their teaching more relevant and interesting; and some, who began by being critical or hostile have developed an interest which has led them to further study—sometimes these in the end, become the best teachers of the subject in school. Still others have at least learned to be less dogmatic and intolerant; they have gained something from free discussion, and have come to see that religious studies are intellectually demanding. So much for the basic course.

Of the colleges that replied to my questionnaire forty-eight offer subsidiary or second main courses, the numbers of students taking these being rather greater than those taking main courses in these colleges. The timetable time spent on them varies from one and threequarters to four hours a week over two years. The students taking these courses have chosen to do so, and can therefore be assumed to have some initial interest in the subject, and, unlike the curriculum or basic course, this one is examined and forms an essential part of the final assessment of the student. In some colleges the course offered appears to be a modified version of the main course and is mainly academic in character; in others much more time seems to be spent on the professional side of the course, practical work being carried on in schools and attention being given to visual aids etc. A number of colleges refer to Goldman's work, and appear to be spending an increasing amount of time on the study of children's development and needs.

The main or advanced main course is essentially an academic one, its chief purpose being the further education of the student, who will spend about a third of his total time in college studying this subject. (Typical timetable allotments range from four hours a week in the first two years and six hours in the third year, to nine periods a week all through the three years.) Students have chosen this subject voluntarily, and in many colleges selection of candidates is made on the basis of the main subject chosen. Although the purpose of the course is the further education of the student, it is from this group of students that future specialist teachers will come. It must be emphasized, however, that not all the students who take main religious knowledge are potential specialist teachers. Many colleges interpreted the 'Balance of Training' circular of a few years ago in such a way that only those taking main courses in science or physical education could train as secondary teachers; and those taking religious knowledge might take junior-secondary courses, but would more often be preparing for work in primary schools. The number also includes far more women than men, and now that earlier marriages are the custom we know that the initial teaching life of women is very limited; while it is hoped that many will come back to teaching when their children are older, it needs stressing that refresher courses will be needed if they are to be adequately equipped. The preponderance of women would appear to be not simply because women are more interested in the subject, but because girls' schools seem to have made better provision than boys' for it to be taught throughout the school at an adequate level.

This leads to a consideration of the criteria by which a main subject is chosen. In most academic subjects colleges usually expect that the student will have studied his subject to Advanced level before coming to college, but this is not usually the case with religious knowledge. If such a demand were to be made many of the best students in the courses would be eliminated and there would be hardly any men qualified to take the course at all. But apart from the shortage of supply, many of the colleges express considerable doubt about the wisdom of asking intending students of religious knowledge to take 'A' level at school. One lecturer writes:

Some who have gained 'A' level qualifications at school speedily withdraw from advanced classes at college. They expect to have more of the same thing they have experienced at school viz. close study of biblical set books. These students find themselves puzzlingly all at sea with quite elementary doctrinal courses such as 'The Person of Christ' studied in such an elementary introduction as *Creeds in the Making* (Alan Richardson S.C.M. paper back). Many training college students do not seem to have been prepared for extending their studies and show alarm at the introduction of such fresh studies as the philosophy of religion and Christian ethics.

And another:

In my opinion an interest and keenness to teach the subject are more important than previous academic qualifications. An enthusiastic student, prepared to work, will make up ground not previously covered. 'A' level qualifications would be a useful start for advanced main work, but good qualifications in English or history would be equally useful.

Another lecturer suggested that some students who had taken 'A' level at school, chose the subject at college because they thought it was an easy option; in this they speedily became disillusioned! There are other students who choose the subject because they are possessed with strong evangelizing zeal; only too often these begin with a somewhat narrow theological viewpoint and they are distressed by modern criticism; if they are prepared to be educated and come with a reasonably open mind, they can do very well; but if they come with a closed mind, hanging on to their fundamentalist views, they are not the best people to send into the schools to specialize, and they are often extremely difficult members of a tutorial group in college. At a recent discussion I attended in Manchester, one headmaster claimed that too often religious teaching failed because it was given by people who were not themselves convinced and practising Christians, with a real enthusiasm for the subject; but I suggest that religious zeal and conviction are not enough. The teacher must be able intellectually to meet the questions and needs of adolescents; and he cannot do this if his mind is closed or if he is too easily shocked. Indeed his own certainty, if it is the kind of certainty that has never been questioned, may be an actual stumbling block to his pupils. (This is illustrated by the attitude of students in basic courses; I remember the sigh of relief that went round one such group when, in the course of discussion, I said that while I could say with complete certainty that I believed in the Resurrection, I was still in a state of agnosticism about the Virgin Birth!) Main courses, in so far as they are designed to train teachers of religious knowledge, must therefore aim at giving knowledge and combining enthusiasm with a readiness to listen to other points of view.

There is certainly no doubt that the courses fulfil the first of these aims; the academic standard is high. Syllabuses include Old Testament, New Testament, Church history, Christian doctrine, philosophy of religion, in some cases New Testament Greek, and, in at least one, Hebrew. Some students in some colleges take external examinations such as the London or Cambridge Diploma in Theology, in addition to the college certificate examination, but with the introduction of the new B.Ed. degree this practice may not be continued. Some anxiety has been expressed lest the planning and examining of courses for the new degree should rest too much with university departments of theology and be too academic. For instance, while there are students who can undoubtedly profit from a study of New Testament Greek, there are others, who may reach an adequate examination standard in this, but who can only do so by spending a disproportionate amount of time on a subject in which they can never go very far, to the possible neglect of at least equally important professional aspects of their work. Indeed I believe that the main problem for those concerned with main or degree course work is to help students to translate the knowledge and insights they are themselves gaining, into teaching which is meaningful and relevant in school. While it is true that main courses are principally intended for the student's own education and development, and also that generally speaking, the students who have the greatest confidence in teaching are those who have really studied their subject in depth and who have some real scholarly knowledge of it, yet I believe there is a danger that we may forget that our task is not quite the same as that of the universities. Our students are preparing from the outset to be teachers and should be continually aware of the educational value and implications of their studies; it might be a good thing if main course students were involved rather more than they appear to be, as an integral part of their course, in experimental work in schools. Some colleges do appear to devote a little time during the main course to work in schools, and of course all students have some opportunity of teaching their subject during periods of school practice; but the following is a fairly typical comment from the replies that have come in: 'The main course is a study of the subject as a discipline without reference to work in schools.' It is generally agreed that one of the most valuable features of the main course work is the long essay, written by the student on a subject of his own choice which he is frequently able to discuss with an external examiner. Would it not be possible to devise, as a parallel to this either individual or group work in schools, which would enable the student to discover more clearly what material can be taken at different stages and how it may be made relevant, so that the kind of lack of theological and psychological understanding revealed by Dr Goldman's research may be avoided in the future?

Finally the picture of what is being done in the colleges of education would not be complete without reference to the supplementary course offered by a small number of colleges. This course is for qualified teachers, and is at present available only to those who had a two year training. When the three year course was introduced the theory was that colleges would be able to achieve as much in a main course as had previously been achieved in a supplementary year. This I believe to be a mistake. Candidates for a supplementary course can be selected from those who have already done reasonably well in an initial training course, and their interests are more stable than those of students entering straight from school. Moreover a year of full-time post-certificate study gives opportunity for concentration and depth of study not present even in the present main course. In the past students sometimes stayed on for a third year at the end of their two year training. Now such courses must be deferred courses and this is a good thing. This is perhaps best illustrated by a comment from a former student who did the end-on course; she writes: 'After having taught for two to three years there are many questions I would like to ask and topics to discuss, the existence of which I was not aware previously.' And another makes the same point: 'I would like to do the course again *now* with some teaching experience behind me and I would gain, I think, even more from it.' While a third, a man who had had some years teaching before returning for the supplementary year writes:

The supplementary course was most valuable in that I was able to view the work done from the classroom point of view, and all the time kept asking myself how I would apply what I was seeing and hearing. During my four years of teaching I had realized that there were many aspects of religious education about which I knew so very little and the extra year provided me with the opportunity of spending time in reading and thinking about the subject. In particular I wanted to consider ways and means of making religious education a living issue to the pupils. I had realized that a purely academic approach was of little value to the average and below average child: something more was needed and I was not sure what that something was. On the course I was able to follow my own inclinations, without the limitations of studying for external examinations. This enabled me to spend time talking with others in the schools and discussing with them common problems and the ways in which they were overcoming them. I think that the main value of the course was to be found in having time to read, to think and to discuss many aspects of religious education. ... What was also of real value was that the course served a dual purpose: it catered for the more open needs of people like myself whilst at the same time preparing students for the Diploma in Theology if they wished to take the exam.

(This man is now doing some very interesting practical experimental work in a school in Lancashire.)

This letter makes clear one of the chief characteristics of the supplementary course: because numbers on the course are usually fairly small (one college once had as many as thirty students taking it, but the numbers more usually range between six and twelve) work can be individually planned to meet the needs of the students; some courses prepare students for a variety of outside examinations ranging from the London Certificate in Religious Knowledge to the London Diploma in Theology; all of them have some method of assessment for a supplementary certificate awarded by the institute of which the college is a part. These courses have been one of the most valuable sources of supply of specialist teachers and it is very much to be regretted that they now appear to be dying out from lack of demand. The numbers in the present year are very small indeed, and of the colleges who have provided a course for some years, one reports that they have only one candidate for next year and another they have none at all. There appear to be several reasons for this state of affairs; one is that the course can only be made available to teachers who took a two year course and is not available for those who have already had three years; as time passes there are likely to be fewer and fewer two year trained teachers applying; secondly, in the present shortage of teachers, some authorities appear to be much less willing to second teachers for courses for religious knowledge than for science or physical education; thirdly, although teachers can be seconded on full salary for the year, there is still financial hardship for the married man with a family, who has to keep his own home going and support himself away from home during the year; and as the supplementary certificate earns no salary increment there is, financially, a positive disincentive to taking it. I believe that the key to the problem of getting more adequate religious teaching in schools lies in the continued and increased provision of supplementary courses and I should like to conclude by developing this point a little.

May I remind you once again that until 1944 very little

provision had been made for the training of specialist teachers
of religion, and not all schools have even yet seen the need for
the appointment of specialists; this is particularly true of boys'
schools where the claims of science and mathematics, in a
limited staffing ratio seem to be much stronger in view of the
constant pressure to fill the science departments of universities
and Colleges of Advanced Technology. Unless there are good
specialist teachers in the grammar schools there is unlikely to
be a very large supply of good candidates wanting to specialize
in religious knowledge in their initial training, and the
numbers for the present main courses will only be increased
marginally. Moreover real interest in religious studies and an
awareness of their value is something which often only comes
with maturity. Many thoughtful teachers, after they have been
brought face to face with social and ethical problems in school
and have become conscious of their own inadequacy as teachers
of religious knowledge are anxious to become better equipped
for their task. Experience in interviewing such candidates
suggests that in the main two types of courses are needed; the
first, like most of the present supplementary courses, should
be for those who already have a reasonable background of
biblical and theological knowledge, but who feel the need for
further, more intensive study and for time to think out, discuss and try out new methods of teaching. The second is needed
for those whose background is at present almost negligible,
who have come to feel this lack and who genuinely want to
prepare themselves to do their job more adequately, not necessarily as full specialists, but as class teachers responsible for
some teaching of religion in schools. It seems to me that the
right place for these courses is in the college of education rather
than in the university or theological college, for here the
students are constantly meeting others preparing to teach other
subjects and can have opportunities of discussing common
problems with them, and can see their subject not in a water-
tight compartment, but as it is related to the rest of the life
and work of the school. (In one college I know well, useful

discussions have sometimes been held between students taking a supplementary course in religious knowledge and those taking a supplementary course in science, and both groups have, as a result, been forced to examine some of their presuppositions more closely.)

Dr Hilliard, in an article in *The Times' Educational Supplement* of April 6, 1965 rightly pointed out that 'Religious teaching has not been tried and found wanting. It has just not been properly tried.' At least one of the main reasons for this is that there have not been enough teachers to do the job. It must be remembered that we are not just being asked to cater for the specialist needs of a few children, but for teaching which must be given to all; and we therefore need more adequately trained teachers than for almost any other subject. A more generous provision of supplementary courses, with adequate incentives for taking them, would, I believe, be the first step in meeting this need. As the impact of these teachers is increasingly felt in the schools, they in turn may inspire more candidates to choose religious knowledge as their main course in college; for these students the colleges perhaps need to give a little more thought to the vocational aspect of their work. From these two groups many of the future specialists will come, though not all main course students will be specialists, and the needs of the primary schools must not be forgotten. Students taking subsidiary courses are also being usefully prepared to take some share though not as full specialists in religious teaching in school. But when one considers the claims of all the other subjects in the curriculum it seems unlikely that more than a minority of students will be taking religious knowledge except in a general or professional course. How far should these courses be compulsory for all students? And what should be their main emphases? In Scotland, where the legal position of the subject is different, where there is no conscience clause for teachers, but also very little provision for the training of religious instruction specialists, there is no doubt about this. All students take a general course in order to help them to teach, and it has therefore a very strong emphasis on material for teaching and on teaching method. If this kind of basic course were universally adopted in England, either much that is at present valuable in the present basic courses in encouraging students to think out and discuss their own problems and their own personal philosophy would have to go, or more time would have to be found for it. This problem of adequate time is, of course a perennial one in the colleges and one that each college must work out for itself. Perhaps some time could be found for a discussion course of this kind in the third year when subsidiary and general courses have been completed, and when students are more mature and more ready to consider philosophical questions. But I know that in some quarters at least this suggestion would produce loud cries of protest because of the fear of cluttering up the third year just when we have succeeded in getting it clear for intensive work in the main course and in education. Perhaps the answer is to bring this course under the umbrella of education and so to get a larger number of college staff involved in it. This must, I think, be left as a point for discussion !

CHAPTER VI

THE TRAINING OF TEACHERS
OF RELIGIOUS EDUCATION

(b) *The University Departments of Education*

FREDERICK HILLIARD

Introduction

The importance for the whole future of religious education of
what is happening in this area of teacher education can scarcely
be exaggerated. It is, of course, true that a certain number of
teachers who have studied divinity to main or advanced level
in colleges of education seek and sometimes secure posts in
grammar schools or comprehensive schools where they will be
teaching young people of above average ability. Yet it is for
teachers with degrees in divinity or a diploma in theology or
religious education, that heads first look to fill posts which
involve the teaching of these children.

It is also obvious that it is from these children that future
teachers themselves will be largely drawn. For it is they who
will mainly provide the undergraduates in the universities and
the students in the colleges of education who are to be
tomorrow's teachers. The quality of the specialist teachers of
religious knowledge in this segment of the country's schools
will thus in turn help to decide the quality of future teachers
of divinity—at all levels of education.

From every point of view, therefore, it is vastly important
that there should be a good supply of teachers with academic
qualifications of degree or diploma level forthcoming from
university departments and institutes of education. The quality
of divinity teaching in all the schools depends on this.

I would wish to make it clear that in stressing this point I am not forgetting that the semi-specialist teacher of religious knowledge has an important contribution to make to religious education in the schools. He most certainly has. Every secondary school, however, and especially every grammar and comprehensive school, ought to have at least one specialist teacher to organize, supervise and advise on the work of religious education as a whole—someone to whom the semi-specialist may turn for guidance and from whom advice can be forthcoming as occasion arises.

Nor am I unmindful of the fact that in the case of religious education above all, qualities additional to the merely academic knowledge of divinity are called for. It will be generally agreed that maturity, experience of life and broad sympathies are vital if a teacher of religion is to gain the respect of adolescents and help them to see the relevance of Christianity to life as it is being regarded and lived in this second half of the twentieth century.

Maturity, experience of life and broad sympathies are not, however, and never can be, substitutes for sound academic knowledge of divinity; they must be complementary to it. At the present time, more than ever in the past, an effective teaching of Christianity can be done only out of a sound knowledge of biblical and historical theology and the facts of Christian history. In the last hundred years or so biblical studies have undergone the greatest revolution in the course of the Bible's whole existence. Christian beliefs are interpreted nowadays very differently from the manner in which they were understood in 1865. Vast developments have occurred in the relationships between the various branches of the Christian churches. The rapidity of modern communications has brought the non-Christian religions of the Middle and Far East into closer touch with the countries of Europe and the New World whose major religious tradition has been that of Christianity (and, to a lesser degree, Judaism). Teachers therefore need to know more about these other great religions.

In any case, it is obviously important that religious educa-

G

tion in grammar schools and schools with grammar-type classes, should be seen by staff and pupils alike to measure up intellectually to the standards of the rest of the teaching. Though the discipleship of the intellect is but one part of all that is involved in full Christian discipleship, it is an exceedingly important aspect for young people who are learning to think fairly deeply and for many of whom Christianity is bound to be subjected to rigorous scrutiny on the intellectual level. Their teachers of religion will be judged in part, even if not by any means wholly, by the extent to which they are seen to be as scholarly as those who teach them in other fields of their studies. All this becomes yet more important when sixth form courses include GCE 'A' level courses in religious knowledge—a topic to which we shall return a little later on.

What contribution then, in purely numerical terms, are university departments and institutes of education able to make to the supply of specialist or semi-specialist teachers of divinity who can be expected to fill posts in grammar schools or in schools with grammar-type groups or streams?

Figures supplied for the current academic year,[1] and which seem to be fairly typical of recent years, present the following picture.

In the university departments of education in England and Wales there are seventy-five students with degrees in theology pursuing the post-graduate education course.

There are also forty-two students with degrees (joint degrees and general degrees) which include theology.

There are approximately 350 students (the figures here are not exact) with degrees in subjects other than theology who are attending courses in religious education.

If we therefore limit the category of 'specialist' teachers of religious knowledge to students with a full degree in divinity or biblical studies, about seventy/eighty become available to the schools each year.

[1] For which I am indebted to colleagues in the university departments and institutes of education.

This is however, probably too narrow a definition of the category, for many students with divinity as part of a joint honours or a general degree can and do make effective specialist teachers. If we extend the category to include them also, we get a total per annum of about 120.

To this number has to be added a small group of graduates with theological or part-theological qualifications who go directly into the schools after graduating. There are also a number with general degrees which include divinity who have taken a four-year concurrent degree and teachers certificate course in one of four London colleges of education—strictly outside the province of this lecture but they have to be included if our number of potential specialist teachers is to be realistic. For the same reason we have also to take into account (a) those who complete full-time, one year courses for a Diploma in Religious Education which at present are available in three university institutes of education—Leeds, London and Nottingham. Typical numbers in recent years here have been between twenty and twenty-five. (b) Those who take part-time and external degrees and diplomas in theology, such as the London B.D., and Diploma in Theology and the Lambeth Diploma.

Adding together the numbers and approximate numbers from all these various sources, it seems reasonable to assume that about 170/180 specialist teachers become available to the schools each year.

I have not been able to secure an accurate break-down of these figures into men and women. It seems fairly clear, however, that the proportion of women is considerably greater than that of men—probably at least two thirds women to one third men. And it looks as though this will continue to be the case— at least until such time as ladies are generally permitted to wear the feminine equivalent of the clerical collar!

Now there are two significant facts to be noted in connection with these statistics. First, that the total of potential specialist teachers of religious knowledge has somewhat improved in recent years as compared with the situation which obtained in the ten years following the passing of the Education Act of 1944. A Joint Four enquiry, for example, made in 1950 revealed that 312 out of 674 grammar schools had no full-time specialist teacher of religious knowledge.[1]

But, second, and more important, that the total is still well below the level in comparable or nearly-comparable fields, e.g. history, geography, music and art.

If we take the initial training courses in the London Institute of Education this year as being fairly typical for this particular purpose, the following facts emerge:

Specialist	historians	60
Specialist	geographers	52
Specialist	musicians	53
Specialist	artists	57
Specialist	theologians	10
(adding Diploma in Religious Education[2])		12

Thus potential religious education specialists represent only about one fifth (or including Diploma in Religious Education students just over one third) of potential specialist teachers in these other nearly-comparable fields.

Another method of checking the estimate of the proportionate output of potential specialist divinity teachers is to see the total in university departments of England and Wales this year as a percentage of the total number of students in those departments—approximately 120 out of a total of 3,661 (this last figure excludes music students at the London Institute), or just over 3 percent.

Viewed therefore, from any angle that we care to take, there can be no doubt whatever that the number of potential specialist divinity teachers continues, in spite of some improvement in recent years, to fall well below the level needed if religious education is to be effectively presented in the schools, streams or

---

1 See *Religious Education in Schools*, a report of the Institute of Christian Education, London 1954, page 56.

2 But the number of Dip.R.E. students is twice as large in London as elsewhere.

groups in which abler children are going to be educated in the next twenty years.

But the shortage of new teachers is, of course, only one factor. The other is the shortage among existing teachers. The recently published report of an inquiry undertaken jointly by the British Council of Churches and the National Union of Teachers into religious education in secondary schools reveals some significant facts here.

Its category of 'Specialist Teacher' is probably too wide but if we give it a broad definition and include in it the teachers who have (a) a degree which includes divinity or (b) a qualification gained either through full-time or part-time study, we discover the following situation in the grammar and comprehensive schools of the random sample, and schools with a grammar-type stream or group : — In thirty-three schools of this type—

twenty-three teachers had a degree including divinity

fourteen teachers had a qualification in divinity or religious education gained through full-time or part-time study

(some of these last might in fact have attained a standard little in advance of GCE 'A' level)

eight comprehensive schools had seven teachers with degrees including divinity and seven teachers with some other qualification

twenty-one grammar schools had fourteen teachers with degrees including divinity and six teachers with some other qualification

six grammar schools had NO teacher with any qualifications in divinity or religious education

NO comprehensive schools were without at least one teacher with one or other type of qualification

For a total of 24,441 children in these thirty-three schools, there were thirty-seven 'specialist' teachers

This is a proportion of one 'specialist' teacher to 660 children. Assuming that one such teacher can teach a maximum of 375 children (on a basis of two periods a week for each class of thirty children, and teaching twenty-five periods a week)[1], this sample suggests that there appears to be an existing shortage of specialist teachers of religious knowledge of at least 40 percent.

It is, then, I think, abundantly clear that the total of specialist teachers in the schools needs to be nearly doubled in the next ten years, and that the output of new specialist teachers from university departments and institutes of education needs to be trebled, if we are to hope for any solid improvement in the quality of the religious education to be given to our abler pupils. Only a concerted effort on the part of the churches, the schools themselves (in which potential teachers can be attracted to the importance of good teaching of religion), and the Department of Education of Science (in stressing the importance of the need for increasing the supply of specialist teachers) would be likely to achieve anything approaching such an increase. It is greatly to be hoped that such an effort will be made, for without an improved supply of informed and enthusiastic teachers of religious education for our abler children especially, the prospect for the next twenty years will be dismal indeed.

It is worth recalling at this point that this problem is one which the provisions for religious education in the 1944 Act both created and yet at the same time helped incidentally to meet—at any rate, up to a point. The fact that religious education became compulsory in all schools created an immediate demand for several thousands of good teachers of religion. By the same token, religious education became a more clearly defined area of general education in which teachers in the schools could look forward to a useful career and to the prospect of increased responsibilities with commensurate financial rewards (a factor not to be ignored just because it happens to

[1] But if he is to get to know the children well, this number is clearly too high.

be religion rather than mathematics, history or English with which the teaching is concerned! The labourer is worthy of his hire and even clergymen working in parishes are now thought likely to be more effective clergymen if they are paid a reasonable stipend). All this, moreover, has in turn encouraged colleges of education to provide better-staffed and numerically adequate departments of divinity. And with only three exceptions, the staffs of university departments of education also now include at least one person, full or part-time, with a theological qualification and experience of the teaching of religion in schools.

This state of affairs has come about very largely as an indirect result of the more clearly defined and important position given to religious education in the 1944 Act and the consequent efforts made by the Department of Education of Science, and by the LEA's to ensure a better provision for religious teaching.

In stressing the urgent need for a further advance in all these areas of teacher education, I shall not then, I hope, be thought to be unmindful of what has been done since 1944. It is excellent so far as it goes. But it will not go anything like far enough to meet the needs of the next twenty years. A renewed effort is now urgently called for.

We must now turn our attention to the aims and content of the courses for these potential specialists in religious education during their year in a department or institute of education. I can speak authoritatively, of course, only about what is done in the University of London Institute of Education, which combines the functions both of a department and an institute. But I have no doubt that what is attempted in London will be typical in many respects of what other departments and institutes try to do. I propose first to speak of the courses for graduates in theology, then of the subsidiary courses for those with degrees in other subjects, and finally about the Diploma in Religious Education course for serving teachers.

The amount of time available for religious education in a

post-graduate education year is limited, as it is for graduates in all subjects, to about one third or one quarter of the total time. This includes the considerable proportion of the twelve weeks or so of teaching practice which is largely, though not exclusively, spent learning to teach religious knowledge. In London we regard it as essential that potential religious education specialists should learn to teach a second subject, even if only for three to four periods a week. For them, as well as for the beneficial effects it can have on their whole standing in the eyes of children and their colleagues in the schools to which they will be going, this seems to us most important.

Our aims in the religious education course can be summed up under five main heads: —

(1) To encourage students to see their work in educational terms.

(2) To get them to give serious attention to the problems and the means of communicating the Christian faith effectively to children and young people who are growing up in the second half of the twentieth century.

(3) To help them to discover how to demonstrate the relevance of Christianity for contemporary life in situations of a personal, social and international character.

(4) In all this, to learn how to maintain consistently high academic standards.

(5) To learn how best to plan and conduct courses for GCE examinations.

I would like, if I may, to explain why some of these aims have seemed to us important.

First, after three years of academic study of any subject, but especially of theology, students' minds have inevitably become conditioned in certain ways—ways which are natural and important for the work they have been doing but not necessarily of the same importance for the work which they will undertake in a school. One of the best illustrations of this is to be seen in the tendency, common to most students at the beginning of the education year, to attempt in the classroom, teaching which is Bible-based in the most obvious sort of way; that is to say, characterized by a textual approach which has become second nature to them during three years of work on Old and New Testament linguistic studies. During their year of educational study and teaching they have to learn to teach *from* the Bible instead of teaching *the* Bible.

Second, the natural atmosphere of a theological department engenders in most students a theological point of view in which the centrality of theology, and of religion, is more or less accepted. However intellectually astringent their course may have been, our theological departments can hardly be regarded as 'open-ended', to use the current jargon. They are frequently staffed by scholars who are also in orders and in some cases serve as centres of study for men intending themselves to enter a ministry. The kind of atmosphere thus created, most graduates in theology who intend to teach have unconsciously absorbed—especially when, as in most cases, they are subjected to a similar kind of influence through their membership of churches and religious societies.

They are, however, being prepared during their year in an education department to teach largely in county schools— schools of and typical of an open society, in which they must learn to justify their presence, and to adjust their teaching of religion, to an essentially educational situation. They have to ask themselves some pretty searching questions about whether religious education is properly a part of general education in a non-denominational school. They must be able to see how an enthusiastic and attractive presentation of Christianity is possible, but which, at the same time, never trespasses across the subtle line which marks off good teaching from preaching.

Third, they have to learn to become interested in education as a worth-while area of serious reading and thinking, as well as keeping alive their theological studies. The former is important if they are not to become narrow subject-minded pedagogues and if they are to feel themselves thoroughly at home in an educational setting. If during their year of education they become interested in the history of education, or comparative education, or educational psychology, sociology or philosophy, then we feel that this part of our aim is succeeding. But if they leave us with no more than a continuing academic interest in theology, we feel that we may not have been so successful at this point.

But fourth, perhaps the most difficult aim of all to achieve is that of encouraging these students to develop the ability to relate Christianity to the life which adolescents are beginning to experience in the second half of the twentieth century. In the nature of the case, experience and maturity are essential here and it is perhaps just these two qualities that are lacking in most young graduates, many of whom have lived, in spite of all that we hear to the contrary, a pretty sheltered existence. And without doubt the teaching of religion is more demanding of maturity and experience than any other aspect of the work that is attempted in school. I sympathize with heads who find it difficult to appoint some of the as yet far from mature theological graduates to teach adolescents about religion. Yet we all had to make a beginning once and at least many of these students show promise of development if only circumstances provide the right contacts and the proper stimulus. I sometimes wish that just as most modern languages undergraduates have to spend a year abroad, so theological undergraduates who are intending to teach religion were expected to do a year abroad working with a body like the Voluntary Service Overseas, or just earning their living for a year in some very ordinary job in cities in Europe or the Commonwealth where they rubbed shoulders with many different kinds of people! The experience would be invaluable.

A word next about academic standards. An undergraduate course in theology should have conveyed to these students a sense of the importance of careful and accurate standards of scholarship and it is important that these standards should be carried over into their teaching and help to stamp it with the best kind of authority. It is not always easy, however, to point students to the direction in which this may most obviously be done, for the reason that a good deal of what goes on in departments of theology has little obvious relation with the teaching of religion to young people in schools. This is a large and delicate matter and I would not want to appear to be suggesting that the academic study of theology should or could be conditioned by the demands of professional work in the field of religion, whether educational or ministerial. Nevertheless, the fact remains that theological studies at the present time are so heavily weighted in the direction of historical and linguistic work, that the gulf to be bridged between the academic study of theology and the task of communicating Christianity to young people is probably wider than it is with any other field of study which has found its way into the school curriculum. There are times, indeed, when the utterances of some Old and New Testament experts in the universities appear to imply that the Bible was written by theologians for theologians! All this makes the task of those of us who have to help students bridge the gap, one of considerable difficulty.

The 'Liberal' theology of the first quarter of this century, and the Barthianism and biblical theology which succeeded it, for all their defects, in their different ways certainly had an important practical and fairly easily understood word to say to ordinary folk who were, or could become, interested in the Christian gospel. I am by no means clear whether the same can be said of the majority of the work which goes on in university departments of theology at the present time. They badly need to recover a sense of their obligation to help to interpret Christianity in terms which the ordinary, intelligent layman can understand. This is especially the case where most of the undergraduates who study in them are going to be, not specialist academic theologians, but general practitioners, either in schools or in the ministry of one of the churches.

The teaching task of the graduate in theology who is going

into a school is probably easiest, in one respect at any rate, when he is teaching for GCE examinations, and especially for advanced level. For he can then conscientiously and usefully bring to bear more directly upon his work some at least of what he has been imbibing during his undergraduate years.

The value of this aspect of his work is, of course, potentially great. He will be mainly teaching young people who may well be hoping to carry on with further study of divinity at main or advanced level in a college of education, or for a degree in a university. In common with his colleagues doing other sixth-form work, he has the opportunity of laying the foundations of good scholarship and of showing his pupils what is involved in becoming a student of the subject. The importance for sixth-formers of this bridging of the gap between school and college or university work has to be made crystal clear to the potential religious education specialist during his education year.

There are, of course, those who decry work for GCE examinations, especially in divinity, on the ground that it tends to take the soul out of religious education for young people at a time when, above all, questions connected with religion need to be considered in a deep and intimate sense which, they argue, is the antithesis of the business of delving into historical detail and the minutiae of literary and textual criticism.

This point of view seems to me to be based on a false premiss. Those of us who have probed even more deeply into the details of theological studies know that, at their best, they constantly interact with the deeper and more intimate movements of the mind and heart. In the hands of a capable sixth-form teacher, religious education in the profounder sense goes on subtly but significantly, with, and even through, the painstaking, detailed studies which are connected more directly with the advanced level syllabus he is following.

You will be aware that in recent years the number of candidates offering divinity at advanced level has grown quite remarkably.

		Entered			Passed	
	Boys	Girls	Total	Boys	Girls	Total
1956	342	851	1193	228	669	897
1963	1011	2290	3301	619	1587	2206

An increase of almost 200% in seven years.

This is encouraging from all points of view but means, in turn, that our courses in religious education for divinity specialists must find time for the adequate consideration of this important part of their work.

Quite as important, in their way, as the courses for potential specialists, are the subsidiary courses in religious education provided in university departments for graduates whose main academic qualifications lie in some field other than theology. These are the folk who will probably take a few lessons in religious knowledge, probably in the lower or middle sections of the grammar and comprehensive schools. Their knowledge of biblical studies will usually be rather limited, as will also be their acquaintance with Christian doctrine and church history. So one of the main aims of the course provided for them must be to get them started on at least some basic reading in these three fields.

There is a sense, of course, in which some basic study of Christian doctrine, biblical and historical, is quite as fundamental as their study of the Bible itself. For only as they are able to teach the Bible against a background knowledge of Christian doctrine will they be able to teach it with insight and assurance. Certainly, however, these subsidiary courses can be only partially effective if they concentrate almost exclusively on classroom methods and techniques of religious education and fail to stimulate in the students a lasting determination to begin and go on with a systematic study of theology itself.

Finally, a word, even if all too brief, about the important work which is being done towards the education of specialist teachers through the Diploma in Religious Education courses in three university institutes of education.

The aim of these courses is inevitably more comprehensive

than that of the courses we have been considering so far. The students come to them with at least five years' experience of teaching, often of religious education itself. They have become conscious of the need for a deeper knowledge of the Bible, Christian doctrine and church history, and of effective methods and techniques of religious education in schools, as a result of the teaching they have been called upon to do. The course has therefore to attempt, within the limited period of three terms and two short vacations, to introduce them to the most important aspects of theological studies as well as enable them to consider religious education itself.

It would, I am sure, be a mistake to sacrifice reasonable standards in the basic fields of theological studies in order to cover a wider range. In London, at any rate, we have concentrated on the Bible and one optional subject, either doctrine, church history or world religions, and tried in them to reach something like final general B.A. in theology standard. We have also given an important place to a consideration of the principles and methods of religious education in schools. A long essay is also required of each student on an educational topic of the student's own choice but subject to the approval of the examiners. We believe that this essay forms a very valuable part of the year's work. It gives students the chance of reading in some depth within a narrow field and of formulating their own opinions on some topic of current significance or of practical importance in the work to which they will be returning.

Over the years we have been impressed by the keenness and hard work which marks the work of the students in this course. Their letters after they have returned to school leave us in no doubt as to the value and importance of this type of course for those teachers in the schools who are having to carry responsibilities for religious education for which they have had all too little preparation and knowledge. I have no doubt that the experience of those who conduct parallel courses in the other two institutes of education is similar.

How are we, then, to see this whole area of work which I

have attempted to describe, on occasions such as this when we try to stand back from it and take stock of it? That for all the efforts that are put into it in departments and institutes of education up and down the country, it represents a small contribution in comparison with what is really needed—that is, alas, all too clear. It wants multiplying, in numerical terms, as I have suggested, at least three times. In itself, however, it is as important as anything that is going on in the whole field of religion in this country. These 'lay theologians' are to come into contact with a far wider number of young people, representative of a genuine cross-section of the whole community, than will be touched by any other agency concerned with religious education. And from their ranks some of the more influential adults of tomorrow will be drawn. Our efforts are directed towards helping religious education specialists to translate older and also contemporary interpretations of the Christian tradition into forms which constitute a genuine religious challenge to young people at a time when that tradition seems to have lost much of its strength and attractiveness. Between a so-called 'new theology' that is far more negative than positive, on the one hand, and a preoccupation in university departments of theology with questions of mainly historical and linguistic detail on the other, our task could hardly be more difficult. But at least it is invigorating and so obviously of crucial importance that we must count ourselves fortunate indeed to have been entrusted with it.

CHAPTER VII

CHRISTIAN EDUCATION AND CHRISTIAN UNITY

THE BISHOP OF LONDON

That it is possible to write a paper with this title 'Christian Education and Christian Unity' is, in itself, highly signficant. Not many years ago the issues of the existence of Church schools and of religious teaching in State schools were responsible for bitter controversy between the Church of England, the Roman Catholic Church, and the Free Churches. That these issues have largely disappeared and that the bitterness has gone, are indications of the growth of ecumenical understanding, and the new atmosphere of co-operation between the Churches in the field of education is itself making a definite contribution to the cause of Christian unity.

To understand the original bitterness it is necessary to remember that the Church of England had from the Reformation a legal right to control education. No one could teach without a licence from the Bishop, though by the beginning of the nineteenth century this had fallen into disuse and non-Anglicans had started schools of their own. Nevertheless when State aid for education began in 1833 the old principles and practices remained dominant, and there was grave concern when in 1839 the Committee of the Council on Education was formed, with the implication that the State intended to be its own agent for education. In that year the Earl of Chichester as President of the Home and Colonial School Society moved:

That it is an object of highest national importance to

provide that instruction in the truths and precepts of Christianity should form an essential part of every system of education intended for the people at large, and that such instruction should be under the superintendence of the clergy and in conformity with the doctrines of the Church of this realm as the recognized teacher of religion.

For a number of years the Church of England through the National Society fought to maintain its control over religious education both against the State on the one hand and the Free Churches on the other. In the process the development of education as a whole was retarded. There was bitter and unceasing controversy especially over the Conscience Clause. When in the end the Church of England made the inevitable concession to the dissenting conscience, it was too late: the antagonisms which had been aroused could not be forgotten. The hostility of Free Churchmen is illustrated by a speech of H. P. Winterbottom in a debate in the House of Commons:

It is due no doubt, primarily to the mere existence of the Established Church, intensified as its ends are by the parochial system. The law of the Church and of the land recognizes one man, and one man only, as the authorized religious teacher in the parish—all others are interlopers, trespassers, poachers on his spiritual preserve. And this is further increased by new-fangled Romish doctrines with which we thought England had long since done.

The bitterness of feeling between Protestant Dissent and Tractarian Anglicanism prevented any common Christian action. By 1870, as one historian of this period of education has remarked: 'Not only was the State, in its efforts to be impartial, pushed by the secularists into neutrality between Christian and secular education, but by undermining the religious integrity of the English school system it assisted the isolation of the working classes from organized religion.'[1] And, as Mrs

[1] Burgess *Enterprise in Education*, page 200.

H

Cruickshank[1] rightly comments: 'Perhaps nothing in the educational controversies of the nineteenth century did more to influence denominational bitterness than the Anglican refusal to concede rights of conscience, for it bred deep resentment and distrust which were to rankle in dissenting hearts for many years to come. Herein lay the problem of the single school area, where there was only one school and that a Church school.' And as the same writer[2] has written:

The two societies (the National Society and the British and Foreign Schools Society) representing the fundamental cleavage in religious opinion, were to dominate English elementary education for the greater part of the nineteenth century. Both Societies had the same objective, the salvation of souls and the permeation of all instruction by religion, but whereas the British and Foreign Schools Society, with one conception of religion, advocated simple Bible teaching, the National Society, inspired by a different ideal, insisted on the teaching of the doctrines and liturgy of the Established Church. These conflicting principles led to a bitter and prolonged controversy in which each group accused the other of the most wicked intentions. The fanaticism and intolerance of the age were reflected in the vehemence of the struggle.

The intolerance also extended to the attitude to the Roman Catholic Church which first received grant aid for schools in 1847. The Irish immigration which resulted from the Irish famine of 1845-6 revived old suspicions of Roman Catholics as something foreign and alien to English ways. There was an irrational fear of domination by Rome which persisted for many years and still further aggravated educational controversy.

It is not necessary to go into further details of this sad story of religious intolerance in the nineteenth century. When the

[1] *Church and State in English Education*, page 10.
[2] op. cit. page 2.

twentieth century opened strife between the Churches could still hold back the development of education as it did in the bitter debates which preceded the Education Act of 1902. A radical reorganization of the educational system, especially in the field of secondary education, was clearly and urgently necessary. By this time the Free Churches, led by Dr Clifford, were violently opposed to any rate-aid for denominational schools. The war-cry 'Rome on the rates' roused passionate feelings. In the result the Act of 1902 was a fair compromise which recognized the dual system as a permanent and essential part of the national system of education while local authorities came into being responsible for standards of education in both types of school. But the controversy had done grave harm both to the relationships between the Churches and to the attitude of the nation to Christianity as a whole. As Mrs Cruickshank has written:[1] 'It is hard to forgive the fanatical extremists on both sides who had degraded national education to a miserable quarrel between Church and Chapel.'

The controversies of 1902 gradually died down but the religious issue still got in the way of educational advance as when it caused the failure of Birrell's Bill in 1906—a Bill which might have given England at that time a united and efficient school system. But as Balfour realized at that time the great mass of English people were becoming increasingly indifferent to religious controversy. The children suffered because the religious instruction which should have given unity and purpose to all the teaching was divorced from the life of the Churches. The Churches suffered because their hostility to each other was intensified and in the process they lost the chance to win back the great mass of English working class men and women.

By 1941 the atmosphere had changed not least because the war had revealed the weakness of the national education. While it was clear that without agreement on the religious

[1] op. cit. page 88.

issue large scale educational reform would be impossible Anglicans and Free Churchmen had come to understand each other better. Moreover the majority of English people no longer cared deeply about religion if they cared about it at all. In this new atmosphere, Mr R. A. Butler, as he then was, could use his insight and understanding and infinite patience to good effect. His White Paper was issued in 1943 and was debated without bitterness, and the Bill which followed, though admittedly a compromise, was passed with little difficulty. The Dual System remained as an integral part of the national system of education and religious instruction and worship became compulsory in all schools maintained or aided by the State.

After 1944 the settlement of the religious issues in education has undoubtedly helped the growth of understanding and co-operation between the Churches. Ecumenical goodwill was put to the test in the discussions which preceded the Education Amending Act of 1959. What was at issue was relatively simple—should the State's contribution to capital expenditure on new voluntary aided schools be raised to 75 percent? Without such an increase neither the Church of England nor the Roman Catholic Church could meet the rising costs of maintaining their partnership with the State. At one time it seemed as though the old fears and opposition of the Free Churches might be revived. Representatives of the Free Church Federal Council and of the Church of England met frequently and their outstanding differences were discussed with complete frankness. Even when agreement on the Bill could not be reached they continued to keep close contact with each other. The Church of England representatives also had full consultation with the representatives of the Roman Catholic Church. On one historic occasion the Chairmen of the Church of England Schools Council and the Catholics Education Council were together in meeting a large group of MP's in the House of Commons. As a result of all these frank and friendly discussions between the Churches the debates in Parliament on the 1959 Bill were marked by an absence of bitterness. The grant was increased to 75 percent and the value of the Dual System was reaffirmed.

Perhaps even more important was that the relationships between the Churches became yet more intimate and friendly after 1959. As a result of the preliminary discussions the Minister of Education said that he would welcome the setting up of a Joint Policy Committee of the Churches to which differences and difficulties could be referred. The Churches took action on this without delay and the Central Joint Educational Policy Committee of the Church of England, the Church in Wales and the Free Church Federal Council came into being on October 1, 1959. This Committee in turn encouraged the formation of similar joint bodies throughout England in areas corresponding to the Anglican dioceses. These Committees have worked so well that almost every difference of opinion over the provision of voluntary aided schools has been resolved without the need for intervention by the Ministry of Education. The Joint Committees have also taken the initiative in discussing the whole field of religious education and have, among other documents, produced an agreed statement of Christian doctrine which any teacher in a county school can teach without violating the Cowper Temple Clause.

The Roman Catholic Church has, so far, not been able to take part in the Central Joint Educational Policy Committee, but there has been constant discussion between the Committee and the representatives of the Roman Catholic Church. The friendliness and the frankness of these discussions illustrate the new spirit between the Churches and it is, I believe, without doubt that common thought and action on educational affairs have in their turn assisted greatly in the growth of ecumenical relations.

Mention must also be made of the work of the Education Department of the British Council of Churches. This came into being soon after the Education Act of 1944—while the round table conference was still fresh in the minds of the members of the new British Council of Churches. The Education

Department therefore was given terms of reference which excluded negotiations with the Ministry of Education on behalf of the constituent Churches. Nevertheless the Department has been active in a wide variety of matters concerning Christian education and has made a significant contribution to the cause of united action by the Christian Churches. It has a joint committee with the National Union of Teachers which has done much to create a partnership between the schools and the Churches, and between teachers and clergy and ministers. It also helps to co-ordinate the work of the Christian Education Movement, which was formed in 1965 by a union of the Institute of Christian Education and the Student Christian Movement in schools, the YMCA and the YWCA. The Education Department has an arrangement with the Central Joint Education Policy Committee for the exchange of information.

This brief survey of the developments in the relationships of the Christian Churches on educational questions will have served to show how in 130 years the situation has changed, from hostility and suspicion to understanding and joint action. The indirect contribution to Christian unity is considerable: but is it possible to discern any direct contribution? In 1944 there were high hopes that when the large majority of children had received compulsory religious instruction according to an agreed syllabus there would be a corresponding increase in the desire for Christian unity. These hopes have not been fulfilled mainly because the religious provisions of the Act of 1944 have had little effect in bringing children into the membership of the Christian Churches. It is not the purpose of this paper to discuss the complex reasons for this apparent failure. But it is relevant to remark that we can now see that the Agreed Syllabuses have been more effective in satisfying the views of the Churches than in meeting the religious needs of the children. The revision of the Agreed Syllabuses which is now in progress in a number of areas will, it is hoped, remedy this weakness but the creation of a desire for Christian unity can only be a long-term and perhaps marginal result of religious instruction and school worship.

The great gain has been in the relations between the various churches. Recently the establishment of a Joint Anglican-Methodist Aided School shows one possible pattern of development. The attacks of the humanists and secularists on the whole principle of a compulsory religious element in national education will almost certainly draw the Churches more closely together. But this at least can be said, that there is now nothing in the sphere of education which should aggravate denominational differences or hinder the cause of unity. The educational leaders of the Churches trust each other and have learnt how to think and work together. That is solid gain.

CHAPTER VIII

CONTEMPORARY MOVEMENTS IN PSYCHOLOGY AND THEIR BEARING ON RELIGIOUS EDUCATION

ROY LEE

Psychology is a term applied to a wide area of study. Its many branches sometimes are so divergent that there seems to be little common ground between them. In the space allowed me it is impossible for me, even if I had the knowledge, to survey all that is being done in the various fields. All psychology has some relevance to religious education, but I must be selective and deal only with what bears most directly on it.

What is known as the psychology of religion is simply the application to a limited subject, religious behaviour, of the methods and concepts used in general psychology. Similarly educational psychology studies what is involved in the processes of teaching and learning. Both are of great interest to us in the theme of this conference, but they are only examples of the use of general methods.

The major division in psychology is between behavioural studies and psychoanalysis in one of its many forms. Behavioural psychology uses the methods of statistics, gathering material as objectively as possible on all aspects of human behaviour and seeking by exact analysis of this material to discover the laws of this behaviour. With it, as a special form, is to be coupled experimental psychology, which tries by experiment to get knowledge of particular psychological processes in animals and man. This type of psychology tends to dominate the studies in our universities today. The other type, which I am going to call psychoanalysis—a term which is normally used to describe only the Freudian school—is more closely allied with medicine, having originated from efforts to cure disorders of the mind, but it now extends far beyond that field and is justly entitled to be called a branch of general psychology. My interests and work have been almost entirely confined to that area, but I hope that it is not for that reason alone, but the converse, that I maintain that an understanding of this branch of psychology is needed to improve the aims and methods of religious education.

An excellent example of behavioural research is that carried out by Dr Goldman of Reading University, which I imagine is familiar to everyone present today. By examining a reasonably large number of children he has reached some important conclusions about the capacity of children of various ages to understand teaching about religion. His conclusions may need re-examination, but they can only be confirmed, modified, or refuted, by further research along the same lines, with perhaps more refined techniques and with a greater number of children. But supposing they are true, we have to ask ourselves in what way they affect religious education as it is and as it ought to be.

To suggest an answer to that question I must repeat something which no doubt previous speakers have stressed. There is an ambiguity in the term 'religious education'. It may be interpreted as meaning instruction about religion, passing on information about the history of religion, its ideas and practices. Secondly, it may mean education aimed at making the learner a religious person. The two meanings are not mutually exclusive, for the second undoubtedly implies the first as part of the education. But in undertaking simple instruction we need not have the second aim explicitly in mind. We may just be engaged on an academic exercise. The School of Theology at Oxford, for instance, is almost entirely devoted to linguistic and historical studies in which it is purely incidental what attitude to religion is taken by the undergraduate. He is examined on his knowledge of his subject, not on the kind of life he is living. The justification for this is that the Oxford School is a school of historical studies in theology, not a school of religion. Even the subject 'comparative religion' is largely concerned with comparative theology.

I believe that in schools and churches we confuse the two meanings and as a result we have no clear aim in mind and our methods of education break down. We tend to intellectualize and aim at instruction, vaguely assuming that this will produce religious attitudes and values in the pupils. On the other hand the purpose of school worship seems to be to influence the children towards becoming religious and to provide an expression for the religion they have already attained. The churches certainly want their children made religious and I am going to assume that the general aim of religious education in the schools is the same, except, possibly, when religious knowledge is taken as a subject in the GCE examinations. Whether or not the schools should aim at nothing more than instruction is a further question into which I do not propose to enter.

Dr Goldman's findings, along with much similar research, are important in throwing light on what techniques we ought to use. For instance, he has made it very clear that we have been grossly over-estimating the capacity of children to understand the abstract concepts of religion, and a lot of hard work will need to be done on revising syllabuses of instruction. His work, however, has little direct bearing on the wider aim of making children religious, except insofar as instruction is part of that aim. As I have said, it is an important part, but I wish to say no more about it, since my concern is with how to train children so that they will become religious, and less has been said about that.

Before I leave the field of behavioural psychology, I should draw attention to research such as that of J. M. Argyle[1] in this country or G. Allport[2] in the United States in gathering

[1] *Religious Behaviour*, Routledge, 1958.
[2] *The Individual and His Religion*, Macmillan, P.B. 1960.

observed data about religious behaviour and drawing inferences from it about common elements in different forms of religion, the function of religion in society, or the changing character of the religious beliefs and attitudes of an individual as he grows. In this way we get a picture of the part played by religion in the individual or society. Again, the more research of this kind is done, the more accurate will the picture be. It will, however, be a picture of what happens, and it will be a statistical picture. It cannot give, and does not attempt to give, any explanation of the inner mental processes which underlie the picture which are the effective cause of all that happens. And it will not provide the means of understanding any given individual.

For this, the inner picture of the human mind, we have to turn to the insights into the functioning and structure of the mind which have come from the use of psychoanalysis as a method of exploring it. Here the emphasis is more on the development of the instincts and emotions, the dynamic and genetic side of the mind, than on intellectual understanding. The pioneer work of Freud and his very considerable achievements have been followed by a great army of analysts in many countries. Various schools have sprung up within the movement, some departing from the concepts formulated by Freud, some claiming to have replaced him, some developing his work in areas which he foreshadowed. All are derived from his original work. A survey of the different schools is impossible in the time I have, but perhaps it is unnecessary, since at least there is broad agreement on the basic ideas. In what follows the Freudian principles are adopted to give a coherent description, since it is misleading to mix up the terminology from the different schools of psychoanalysis, particularly those of Jung and Freud.

I shall select four central themes for consideration. They are key matters in relation to religious education and they are very much under discussion by psychologists. They are :—(1) the nature of personality; (2) the growth in the child of ideas of

God and of attitudes towards him; (3) the nature of morality; (4) the empirical character of mature religion.

Personality

The central theme in all schools of analytical psychology today is the nature of human personality. We have returned direct to the question raised by the psalmist: 'What is man that thou art mindful of him, or the son of man, that thou visitest him?'. I say 'returned' because it seemed to many who failed to see the full import of his work that Freud had somehow taken away the personality of man and reduced him to the level of a battleground of biological or impersonal forces. The so-called neo-Freudians in the United States, Erich Fromm, Karen Horney, and the rest, who are laying great stress on personality, seem to claim, or have claimed for them, that they have superseded Freud and returned to the human viewpoint instead of the merely biological.

We ought not to fall into this error, nor should we if we take account of the work of some of our own psychologists, notably Melanie Klein,[1] Winnicott,[2] Fairbairn[3] and Laing.[4] The new emphasis simply brings Freud's work to the next stage, and no one has pointed the way more clearly than Freud himself in his great works, *The Ego and the Id* and *Civilization and its Discontents*, in particular.

It is obvious that the assumptions we make about human personality will shape the aims we have in religious education. It must be confessed that much of what is being done today is still based on assumptions which through ignorance or sheer refusal take no account of the knowledge which has come from psychology. One such assumption is that a person, or the mind of a person, is a kind of immaterial thing, a given unity in itself, acting upon the world and being acted upon in turn,

[1] *The Psychoanalysis of Children* (Hogarth Press).
[2] Collected Papers, *The Family and Individual Development* (Tavistock Publications).
[3] *Psychoanalytic Studies of the Personality* (Tavistock Publications).
[4] *The Divided Self* (Tavistock Publications).

but always from outside. This view has been given some support by the reaction from Freud and emphasis being placed by the neo-Freudians and others, such as Ian Suttie, on the importance of social relationships in shaping the growth of a person. The reaction is, I said, a misunderstanding and is due to a confusion about methodology. Freud himself was not always free from it.

The individual is always in an environment, so it is open to us to study the nature of his relationships with that environment, observing them from outside and inferring from them their causal effect on the state of the individual. On the other hand, we may begin with the individual, examining his state of mind and his reactions to his environment. In this case we work from within outwards. Psychoanalysis began with the treatment of individual patients and therefore adopted the second method. It is still the main line of work with psychoanalysts, even in group therapy, but the growth of social psychology and the influence of behavioural methodologies has led to a wide interest in the social factors which produce the effects in the individuals studied by the other method. It is a question of emphasis. Confusion only arises when the two approaches are seen as rivals and not as complementary to each other. Unfortunately, though no doubt inevitably, the resistance to Freudian ideas which he encountered still prevails and many people fall into the temptation to regard the social approach as a replacement of his ideas, not a development of them. Both are necessary. For some insights the individual approach is most rewarding, for others we gain by using the social.

To understand what a personality is we need to use both. We need to know what is happening inside the mind and we need to see those processes in direct relation with the environment to which they are the reaction. For it is now clear that a personality is always in process of becoming, an expansion of inner psychic forces and the incorporation of the environment. The resultant is to be seen both as structure and function. The structure of personality is very complex, a complexity which is developed from the diverse experiences a growing child must undergo in a normal environment and from the conflicting impulses which spring from within himself and which maintain the structure that is formed. The self which each of us knows within him is only part of his total personality. The ego or 'I' rests upon a far greater body of mental activity which influences behaviour and shapes our character in spite of being thrust out of the ego. The ego is the seat of consciousness but it is not only true that 'we do not know what we shall be', we do not even know what we are. Yet in dealing with human beings, and particularly in education, we must concern ourselves with the whole personality in its becoming and not just with the conscious ego. For that reason religious instruction, which appeals to the reason, cannot be full religious education. The unconscious part of each person is so extensive and powerful that our education must be planned in relation to it as well as to the conscious mind.

The importance of the unconscious is due to the dynamic nature of the mind. Whatever is repressed out of consciousness is not thereby deprived of its energy; it remains active and some means of expression for it is necessary or else a mental breakdown results. The expression that is gained is always a compromise formation, a substitute satisfaction. It may take any of a multitude of forms, even illness. Where the substitute satisfaction has social value and social approval it is called a sublimation. Sublimation requires a whole chapter in itself, and while the foregoing description of it is not exact it is the one commonly used. As sublimations, religion and other social and cultural activities are motivated by energies drawn from more primitive sources, or are little disguised expressions of repressed wishes. Behind all our actions usually lie more than one motive, conscious and unconscious. Even our intellectual interests are directed by emotional urges.

The division into conscious and unconscious sections of the mind is not the only one. Cutting across it there is a three-fold division of the total personality into, in Freudian terminology, id, ego, and super-ego. The id is the source of energy, of desire; the ego is the conscious self, the instrument of action to secure satisfaction of desires; the super-ego is the seat of standards imposed upon behaviour. At this point I only ask you to take note of this complex character of personality, for I shall come back to it to treat it in more detail when I am examining the nature of morality. It is the product of the growth of the individual in his social environment, and, like all growth, may not achieve perfection. Hence we have always to take the conditions of growth into account, adopt the genetic point of view, in seeking to explain personality.

There is one other factor to which I must draw attention before I proceed to discuss the implications of all this for religious education. It seems intrinsic to the human mind to seek to unify its experiences. The chief instrument of unification is the reason, or intelligence. The unconscious exists because it could not be unified with what consciousness had already accepted. What was repressed was too disturbing, too dangerous, too shameful, to be allowed in consciousness, so the attempt had to be made to reject it. The aim of psychotherapy is to bring such repressions back into consciousness in conditions where they may be absorbed into consciousness by a maturer personality. The over-riding effect of this drive for unity is that the mind is always reaching forward to attain something not yet realized. The personality is always in process of becoming. It is the continuing process of actualizing inner potentialities, the attainment of ends aspired to, the synthesis of diverse, perhaps conflicting, elements in the mind, the incorporation of new experiences of the world beyond the self, the springing into being of new impulses and goals of action. The general aim of education is to create well equipped, mature persons; the aim of religious education is make people religious, that is, I suppose, spiritually developed; and the aim of psychotherapy is to restore people to mental health. It is by no means clear that these mean the same thing. Certainly many would dispute it. It is, however, futile to argue about it until we know what the terms mean, maturity, spiritual health, and so on. It is not enough to define them in *a priori* formal terms, we must try to fill them out with a positive content. It is here that psychology can help us.

Let me recapitulate the points we have to bear in mind. Man is a psychic organism endowed with special abilitites and energies which lead him to seek certain ends. He is a growing organism and as he grows the abilities develop and the ends he seeks change as a result of his natural growth and his experience in living. His personality becomes organized into a complex structure and he also becomes divided within himself. The division may or may not be necessary or desirable, but in spite of it there is that in him which tries to hold the diverse elements in a unity, to integrate them to each other. He is not aware of all the processes going on within his mind any more than he is aware of all the functioning of his body, for consciousness belongs only to one part of the complex psychic structure. He is always moving towards the future. Personality is a continual becoming.

In the light of these guides we must examine the growth of personality and what we must look for are directions of growth rather than some postulated state of perfection. What is ideal for today may be unsatisfactory for tomorrow. 'When I was a child, I spake as a child, . . . now I am become a man, I have put away childish things.' But I could not become a man if I had not first been a child. The whole man is all the stages of growth from the beginning until the end, the end, as I believe, which never comes, but is only the limiting point of time and of eternity.

We may trace the growth of an individual in three ways:— (1) in relation to other people or groups of people and the world in general; (2) in the development of the ideas, images, sentiments, aims, which are the tools of the mind; and (3) in the formation of the complex structure of the mind and the tensions between the constituent parts. In this way we see what is required to make an individual person, how the idea of God is formed, and the place of morality in the mind and the nature of its demands. The three lines of development are of course interwoven and enter into each topic. Finally we see that a fresh view of religion emerges from the over-all consideration.

The child begins life as an organic part of his mother, nourished in her womb with all his bodily and mental needs supplied by her. In due course he is thrust out of his haven, or heaven, and now depends on his own organs to secure the means of life. His mother is still almost his whole world. She feeds him, cleans him, protects him from heat and cold and hurt. He needs her love, her company and her attention to him as a person to foster the growth of his mind and to develop the awakening powers of observing, recalling images, learning, desiring, of handling the gamut of emotions which begin to move in him.

The observer sees a growing baby as a personality already developing his own individual character, but the baby himself is not conscious of his separateness for about the first two years of life, not aware that he is a person separate from his mother. All he can be aware of is a confused mass of experiences which through constant repetition gradually take on order and patterns with sub-patterns. On the one side the mother becomes a dominant pattern and on the other he learns the intimacy belonging to the sensations of his body. At some point a division occurs and the baby becomes aware of himself as a person over against his mother. He has reached consciousness of self and now must forever be locked in his own individuality.

It follows from this that the individual person does not begin as an individual complete in himself and enter into relations with other persons from outside them. His individuality emerges from a matrix of experiences in which he is, as it were, living within the pattern that is his mother. She in turn is to him the focus of all his experiences of the world impinging upon him. What he becomes is dependent on his experience of her, on the way she treats him. His human-ness is potential within him, but it has to be awakened and shaped through

I

association with other humans. Brought up by wolves he would become a wolf in character and behaviour, as we know from the study of wolf-children. Our growth is the resultant of our inherited powers and the environment which stimulates them. Each of us has a unique identity, but each of us embodies his environment in the character of his personality as well as in his knowledge. Environment of course includes what all the means of knowledge open to us. Books, pictures, radio, television, art, architecture, music, take us far afield in time and space. Indeed each of us is a unique concrescence, in Whitehead's phrase, of the universe. The universe is immanent in us.

This is of great importance for religion, but before I come to that I must outline the subsequent stages of development. Between two and three years of age he becomes aware of his father as a person, and then of other persons, and this compels him to pass out of the security of his relationship with his mother into a period of intense emotional conflict. This normally ends between the ages of five and seven and his interest turns away from the family to the outside world. In the stable period of childhood he accumulates knowledge and learns to distinguish between reality and fantasy, between fact and fairy story. At puberty he is again forced to leave the security and relative peace of childhood to enter the turbulence that adolescence brings. He has now to find a meaning for life within himself, so this is a period of romanticism, idealism, adventurousness. He has also to find his full independence, so it is also a period of rebelliousness, of criticism of his elders and of current ideas and practices. With adulthood he finds a place in society, but marriage and children bring him into a new state of existence. As he grows older other stages supervene until finally he has to come to terms with death.

The picture that we get from this process of growth has two outstanding features in it. The first is that the growing person increases, if that is the right word, in individuality, in independence and self-reliance. He has repeatedly to break free from an environment which has nurtured him for a time, as in birth and in turning away of his emotional involvement with the family constellation. This breaking free is not merely physical and social, it is also necessary in mental and spiritual matters. To hold him under authority is to defeat his growth. Authority serves for a period to prepare him for further growth. but there comes a time when he must think and act for himself and assume full responsibility for his own life. Each stage of his growth marks a strengthening and enriching of his individuality and at the same time a widening of the area from which he draws the material to feed the growth. He grows by incorporating the world, and especially other people, but he only grows by making it his own. Religious education, therefore, must aim to foster independence. Each individual must become his own authority. This independence must hold even in relation to God. This is the only kind of God worth teaching, a God who wants men to be images of him, not puppets without life of their own, a God who is the source of the urge to growth, who is working in all the processes of the universe to raise men so that of their own freedom, their own will, their own spontaneous desire, they will love and seek to do those things that are of God. He does not want men who will only obey from fear, fear of hell, fear of failure, fear of death. He wants sons who belong to his household, friends and fellow workers who will take their part in his work of creation.

The second feature which stands out in the growth of personalities is that it is always by incorporation of an environment of other persons. It follows that if religion means to be centred on God, religious education requires that the growing person must be in the environment of God. In an abstract sense, a real sense also, we are always in God, since God is the meaning and source of all that is. But God must come to the individual in a personal way. This is not brought about by the recitation of formulas about the personality of God but only by bringing the individual into contact with other persons who have embodied God in themselves. He may meet such persons in the flesh, or meet them through books and all the forms of art. It is not enough to have God as an idea, he must be actualized. We need to live, as de Chardin has so forcefully put it, in *le Milieu Divin*. The trappings of religion are not sufficient, the Church is the blessed company of all faithful *people*.

If maturity and spiritual health mean anything it must be this. It is the embodiment of God in us as human beings; each achieving incarnation in us, becoming divine—in the Christian phrase, 'filled with the Holy Spirit'. But this means that to become divine in this sense is to become fully human, and this is the goal of growth. Religious education, then, must have the twofold aim, to foster independence and to foster community. On the one hand the individual must not be tied down to acceptance of absolute authority in dogma or morals. On the other hand he should be shown the value of what comes from the past, but encouraged to test it from his own experience and insight until he can make it his own or arrive at something better. Rejection out of hand is to cut oneself off from community. Bible, creeds, Church, morals, are material for incorporation by the individual, not outside authorities forbidding his growth. The order of values still remains, 'the Sabbath was made for man, not man for the Sabbath.'

The Idea of God

I turn now to the second area where modern psychology has something to say of importance in religious education. How important it is has been revealed by the widespread interest in the ideas put forward by the Bishop of Woolwich in *Honest to God*. To do him justice, he has only put out in a semi-popular form what scholars have been saying, or implying, for a very long time and neither he nor his publishers anticipated the remarkable interest, both for and against, which his challenge to prevailing notions aroused. He has shown the disastrous consequences of taking the metaphors we use to describe God as concepts to be taken literally. His failure has been to find adequate metaphors to replace those he has destroyed. The human mind needs metaphors or myths as part of its armoury, but it needs also to recognize that a metaphor is a metaphor and not a literal description of an actuality. Metaphors are steps on the way to deeper understanding, and to destroy them may hinder progress in knowledge, not further it.

Dr Goldman has shown that before the age of eleven or twelve years the average child is not capable of understanding the abstract concepts in which the Church formulates its ideas of God and the Christian life. The idea of God is in any case the most difficult of all to formulate and even the philosophers and theologians resort to metaphor when they use terms such as the Absolute, First Cause, Prime Mover, Ground of Being, Creator. It is too much to expect children to have any meaningful grasp of such concepts. But long before they reach the mental maturity required to think about God in general terms they have heard the name. What meaning can they be expected to give it?

According to the principle of apperception, the mind can only take in what previous experience has prepared it to do and the new experience is assimilated to the old and interpreted in terms of the old. This is valid both of reasoning and of feeling. When, therefore, the name God is presented to the child, usually in a context which makes it appear important to the adult and charged with strong feeling tones, the child can only interpret it by the ideas and images, conscious and unconscious, which have been shaped in his mind in the early years. These images have been derived from his relations with his parents.

I have tried to trace in some detail elsewhere[1] the growth of these images, so I shall only summarise them here. Like any other growing thing the mind of a child has to form itself as it grows, partly according to impulses from within and partly in response to influences acting upon it from without. It develops its own tools through experience in the form of mem-

[1] *Your Growing Child and Religion*, Penguin Books, 1965.

ories, images, gestures, language, and with these it meets new experiences, refining the tools at each step. Ready-made tools cannot be put into its hands, if the metaphor will be allowed. They are only usable when they are assimilated to what is already in the mind.

In the first two years of life the mother forms almost all the world the child knows and she is the link that binds all his experiences together. Some of those experiences are highly pleasureable, some are unpleasant—hunger, cold, pain, discomfort, loneliness, and so on. Both sets of experiences are ascribed to the mother, hence the infant forms two opposed images of her, a good image and a bad image. She is the most beautiful being and the source of all delights and at the same time she is the 'terrible mother' described by Jung. When the young child gets to know his father, similar good and bad images are formed of him. In the good image he appears as the great protector, the supplier of all wants, the omniscient, omnipotent being who is the ideal of the son and the aspiration of the daughter. In the bad image he is terrible in his anger, a stern judge, always on the watch to detect wrong-doing and to punish even with death, and all powerful. The images are not realistic reproductions of the parents. They are a function of the weakness of the infant as compared to them and of the intensity and nature of the emotions their treatment has evoked in him. If the emotions have been intense and conflicting the contrasting images will also carry strong emotional overtones, and there is likely to be strong feelings of guilt and insecurity attached to them.

Here ready to hand is a set of images and feelings which seems to fit what the adults mean when they talk about God. The parental images are projected onto God and with them the emotions which were originally attached to the parents. God will be omniscient and omnipotent like the father, the great protector and source of good things, the giver of love and tender care, like the mother, the healer of hurts and the forgiver of sins. Or he will be the all-terrible, the fearful judge who

sees and punishes all offences, demanding unswerving obedience to his commands, or requiring supplication before he will
grant what we want. He elicits adoration, gratitude, fear,
guilt, atonement, self-humbling, in every degree possible. In
whatever guise God cannot help but be interpreted as a powerful person somewhere up in heaven, one being among others
and therefore acting from outside them by mysterious and
magical means. Such a picture is inevitable.

Daily contact with the parents enables the child gradually
to correct his images of them and to substitute observation for
fantasy as a means of appraising them so that the images are
replaced by a more objective knowledge. If the child has developed repressions to any severe extent it is likely that in his
unconscious the images will still be attached to them. But so
far as they relate to God it is difficult for any testing out by
direct experience. The child cannot get at God to verify his
picture of him. God is out of his reach. He can only compare his
image of God with what he is taught and what he can observe
about those who profess belief in God and claim knowledge of
him. He can test God by seeing whether he answers prayers
and gives what the child asks for, and he can reflect over
where God protects him and his family from hardship and suffering. As he gets older, of course, he can examine the lives of
saintly people to see how far they reveal the qualities which
he has associated with God. Supremely he can study the life
and person of Jesus as given in the Gospels. And he can compare religious teaching with the knowledge of the world that
comes to him through history, science, art and literature. But
this is only possible if his repressions are not so severe as to
prevent him thinking freely about God.

In this lies the most difficult of the problems which religious
education has to solve, namely, how to lead the child to a
correct idea of God and to correct attitudes towards him. It is
doubtful whether we know what is the correct idea of God or
are able to live in a right relationship with him if we knew
what it should be. There will always be more to be discovered

about God and to think that at any time we have discovered
the fullness of truth about him is little short of blasphemy.
Similarly it is the experience of those who have been filled with
the Spirit of God that it opens an unending vista of richness
before them yet to be attained. But even granted that we know
in part the nature of God, what he is and what he is like,
that knowledge has to pass through teachers and it would be
too much to hope that they would be free from the repressions,
the distortions of thinking and living, the in-built biases to
which we are all liable.

Further than that, the child may come to school or church
already twisted so that he is hindered from grasping the truth
when it is presented to him. For instance, his first contact with
the world is in the person of his mother. If she fails to give him
dispassionate love, the love he needs to be able to depend on in
all circumstances to give him personal security, if she with-
draws her love when he is troublesome or naughty, so that he
feels that he is not lovable and not wanted, he will be unable
to understand what is meant by the affirmation that God is
love. He will believe that God loves us only when we are good,
and the meaning of the incarnation and crucifixion will pass
him by. In life he will always be insecure and his picture of
God will oscillate between a kindly old man who for reasons of
his own will overlook misdemeanours if you get on the right side
of him and a stern and relentless judge always ready to punish
even the slightest breach of his commandments.

I could not hope to run through all the possibilities of distorted understanding about God. They are infinite. But from
what I have said it should be clear that religious education
does not lie primarily in teaching about God but in the way
the young child is treated. The first five years of life are the
most important, for in them the foundations are being laid,
but no religious teaching can be given in those years. What
can be done is so to treat the child that he will form images
of his parents which will help him later to understand teaching about God, and by unswerving love and concern for his

development to give him confidence in life and towards the world, a confidence which later will grow into faith in God.

This means that both teachers and parents need the right kind of training. I would not venture on the technical aspects of this, but will make two simple points. First, they should be made to realize that they will bring the children to religion more by what their own attitude is to God, to life, and to the child, than by what instruction they give him. Religion must always be lived—and acting out is not living—if it is to be passed on. The second point is that religion is not something apart from the rest of life. It is an orientation of the whole of life and therefore the concepts of God and religion must never be limited to the overt forms of institutional religion or of private piety but must be shown to be significant in all that concerns human life. In other words, science and history, art and economics, are as much religious studies as is theology.

Morality

Another area in which modern psychology has a contribution to make to religious education is that of morality. By this I do not mean that psychology shows us that we should vary some of the accepted moral standards. It is true that some psychologists, or people claiming to speak as psychologists, have advocated, for example, greater freedom in sexual relations than the current moral codes permit. That may or may not be advisable, but I do not want to discuss this aspect of the question. I want to speak about the place of morality in religion and in the personality in the light of what we now know about the structure of the personality.

The old view of conscience was a simple one. Conscience, the seat of morality, was regarded as an innate faculty by which the mind is able to discern right and wrong. It was recognized that conscience had to be educated by reason and authority to stimulate its proper functioning, but in itself it is a God-given organ to guide our conduct. It is a fact of experience, it can be argued, that everyone recognizes the sense of unconditional obligation to do the right when it is known and to avoid the wrong, even when we disobey our conscience. The penalty for disobeying is an uncomfortable sense of guilt which can only be taken away by forgiveness for our wrong-doing and some expiation for it. It is true that this view of conscience raises some difficulties, such as that some people seem to have an extraordinarily strong conscience whereas in others it is weak, that some people are very conscientious over trivial matters and not over weighty ones, and that it is difficult to strike a balance between the absolute obligation of duty and the tenderer attitudes of love. Can God be love and at the same time relentless towards wrongdoing? But ways could be found to soften down these difficulties. What people need is to be educated to what is right and given encouragement and exhortation to do it, with the threat of penalties here or hereafter to discourage doing wrong.

We can no longer look at conscience in this simple way. We now know that personality is not unitary but complex in structure and that what we have been taking as an innately given function is developed in the course of growth. What we call conscience is the tension which prevails between two parts of the complex personality, of which the I which feels the pressure of conscience is one. That which exerts the pressure is the 'super-ego'. On the conscious level it acts as conscience; on the unconscious level it is the repressing force which keeps desires and memories it forbids from coming into consciousness.

The super-ego is developed in the young child somewhere about the age of five to seven as a means of escaping the conflicts which Freud called the Oedipus Complex. It results in the internalization, the introjection, of the authority and power which the parents seemed to the child to be exercising and it embodies these commands which he thought they were giving. It also takes into itself the actual commands, the vetoes, which they did make. In addition, it takes into itself the aggression which from birth onwards the infant found necessary to turn in upon his own desires, particularly aggressive ones, which he had to control as too dangerous and as threatening loss or destruction of love. To this nucleus are added later rules of conduct accepted from parent substitutes or society or evolved by reason working over experience.

The formation of conscience in this way gives many opportunities for mal-development, resulting in scrupulosity, over- or under-developed conscience, selective operation, unbalanced guilt feelings, and so on. A savage conscience can be directed internally or projected outwards to condemn other people. And the super-ego can be highly repressive in the unconscious, leading to distorted secondary effects on the conscious level. All this is now well known and conscience is therefore no longer seen as a safe guide to what is right or wrong. What is not so easy to say is what is a healthy conscience. Some super-ego there must be. Without it a person is a psychopath, lacking any restraining power over his actions and devoid of social responsibility. The question is not merely an academic one. We need to have some idea of what a healthy conscience is and how it is attained so that we may direct religious education to the best ends and in the best way. I will come back to that presently.

Meanwhile I want to draw attention to a division within conscience which is increasingly being recognized and in the light of which some of what I have just been saying needs modification. The distinction is between positive and negative morality. Some moral rules say, 'do this', others say, 'do not do this'. They have been lumped together under the general heading of moral judgement and conscience, but now we see that there is a distinction between them of function that is not explained just by the positive or negative form.

Negative morality is the work of the super-ego. The super-ego was developed as a means to control desires which threatened to bring the ego into the danger of destruction by the parents and it introjected their authority, the introjected image becoming a permanent structure within the total personality. Its function was always negative, forbidding or repressing the desires it opposed, and creating a sense of guilt, conscious or unconscious, when its behests are disobeyed. But there is another function in us which urges us to do things, not to refrain from doing them. This is the work of what is called the ego-ideal, a term first used by Freud fifty years ago, but which he dropped when he discovered the nature of the super-ego and assumed that a positive as well as negative morality could be explained by the latter. So far as morality is concerned the ego-ideal is more important than the super-ego, though it is not always the more powerful.

The ego-ideal is the picture of what we want to become. Its basis is love, not fear, although the fear of losing love enters into it. Our most fundamental spiritual need is to be loved, first by our mother, then by father and afterwards by all people we know; lastly by God. The child forms a picture in his mind of that which he must be to ensure that his mother loves him. It comes from her attitudes to him and from what she tells him. The fear of losing her love is a powerful inducement to obey her. But the young child also sees how wonderful his (or her) parents are and knows his love for them. If therefore he can be like them, beautiful, good, great and powerful, he will be more lovable. So he builds up a picture of what he should be to make sure of being lovable. He is not always conscious of this underlying motive, for the fear of being unloved and unlovable is so terrible that it is usually deeply repressed. If it gets to the surface it can produce profound depression. The ego-ideal is progressively expanded as the growing person gets a wider experience of life and of people. In the last resort it centres upon God, whose love sustains through all things.

The characteristic of the ego-ideal is that it can never be attained, for beyond what we are there always stretches a greater ideal ahead. The super-ego may be so strong that a person may say that he has never done anything wrong, and he may be saying what is close to the truth. Yet such a life may be filled with coldness and lack of achievement, a life of self-righteousness without joy or freedom. The life that is lived under the dominance of the ego-ideal is more likely to be filled with outgoing love in gratitude for the love that is received. It is also likely to be a life of humility, for such a person knows how far short he continually falls from the ideal, yet he is filled with hope because he knows people, and God, believe in him.

So far as religious education is concerned, the lesson is clear. Morals should not be taught as absolute and authoritative and there should be as little emphasis on negative morality as possible. God as judge should give way to God the creator and giver of life, the God who loves us even when we do evil things. He does not seek to punish but to restore, his concern is for our welfare. He puts that before his own dignity or any demand that due respect be paid to his commandments. The latter are meant to help us to find our true selves, to grow into that fullness of being of which we catch glimpses in the ideals we pursue. We should be ready to encourage and praise any positive achievements and to point the way forward to still greater ones. Of course we must be careful not to aim for an ego-ideal that is too far above the actual self. We must be careful too to value the right kind of achievements, not material successes or social triumphs but growth of personality.

The Empirical Character of Religion

In conclusion I would like to draw together what I have tried to say in the areas of life I have been surveying. I sum it up as leading to the conviction that religion is an empirical matter, not one of authority and dogma. God is the great reality, the all-inclusive being, the meaning of all things. You see that I am caught in the pitfall I warned against earlier on. I can put it another way. Religion is a function of the ego, not of the super-ego which is the authority within us. The ego is that part of us which explores the world and which adjusts our desires, our urge to live, our need to grow, to that real world. The only place where it can find God is in that world, by accepting the world, by going through the world to its inner meaning. All that gives knowledge of the nature of the world feeds such a religion, science, art, history, literature. But above all it is in meeting people of rich lives that we penetrate most deeply into the secrets of living.

It is with this faith in life, with this desire to explore the universe, this hunger to find God that we must seek to inspire those who come under our care.

CHAPTER IX

CONTEMPORARY MOVEMENTS IN THEOLOGY AND THEIR BEARING ON RELIGIOUS EDUCATION

DENNIS NINEHAM

Honesty compels me to begin by exposing my almost total nakedness, so far as qualifications for giving this lecture are concerned. It is true that I am the father of four children, all under eighteen years of age, and as such I have, at one remove, been at the receiving end of a good deal of religious instruction in the past ten or twelve years. It is also true that as a governor of more than one grammar school I have heard something of the problems and concerns of those who teach divinity; and that as a governor of a Church Training College I have learned something of the work of those who teach the teachers of divinity. But the nearest I can get to a real qualification is the fact that for a number of years I had the privilege—and it was a privilege—of helping Dr Hilliard with the admirable one-year diploma course he has started in the University of London Institute of Education for teachers who wish to add a divinity qualification to a degree which they already possess in some other subject. This brought me year by year into touch with groups of established teachers who already had some experience of teaching divinity and who reacted variously, but always interestingly, to a year's course of instruction in contemporary New Testament scholarship and criticism. There came a point each year when they were led to reflect on the significance of what they had learned for their past and future teaching, and if there is any truth in what I have to say, it will largely be due to the fact that they usually shared at least some of their reflexions with me.

If, on the basis of this scanty qualification, I have to hazard an opinion about the present situation, I should guess that the best divinity teachers, at any rate in the upper forms of schools, are trying to steer between a Scylla and a Charybdis.

On the one hand there is the teaching they have to do in connexion with examination courses, particularly for 'O' level and 'A' level divinity. The syllabuses usually comprise some set books from the Bible or set periods of biblical history, and these have to be studied in what is essentially a technical manner, linguistically, historically, archaeologically, geographically and so forth; documentary analysis, literary criticism, and the so-called 'higher' criticism are involved. Obviously such courses are none the worse for being rigorous and exacting, and the standards attained are often remarkably high. The problem, however, is that teaching for such courses is only in a rather Pickwickian sense *religious* instruction; not many opportunities are offered for raising specifically religious questions or suggesting the characteristically Christian answers to them. Yet many of the teachers feel that some such opportunities should be offered in the course of anything that can properly be called religious instruction, and I shall give my reasons presently for thinking that they are right.

Meanwhile we are brought to the Charybdis, for it may be replied to what I have just said that most schools provide in the schedules of their upper forms for free discussion periods when any and every question concerning human life and destiny, including religious and moral questions, can be ventilated and discussed. That is true, and no one would want to deny the great value of such periods, whether as a sort of free-expression activity for adolescents or as opportunities for older children to learn how to discuss without becoming emotionally involved in the bad sense, and how to allow even their most cherished convictions to be modified, if that is the way the argument genuinely leads. However, as vehicles of religious *instruction* such periods are in practice of somewhat limited usefulness. The whole atmosphere is one in which each person feels free to express his or her individual opinions on the basis that one man has as much right to his view as another, and if the teacher is to emerge as any more than, at most, *primus*, or *prima, inter pares*, he or she has to be a remarkable person. To show the children that their personally felt convictions and problems are precisely what Christian teaching is concerned with, and what the bearing of Christian teaching on them is, requires both a born teacher and someone who is theologically literate and has had the opportunity for considerable reflexion on his or her theology. In practice periods of this sort are usually taken by people who have no theological training at all; and even divinity specialists often feel that their training has not been of the right kind to enable them to take full advantage of the real opportunity which such periods could often no doubt be made to provide.

It can thus happen that neither of the activities which comes under the umbrella of "religious instruction" really achieves its end; and a child who has had benefit of both may finish up with so hazy a notion what Christianity really stands for as to be unable to pass a responsible judgment upon it. The reason for this state of affairs appears to be partly that the right sort of occasion is not provided and partly that few teachers have the training or background to take full advantage of such opportunities as do occur.

At this point it may be useful to enquire briefly how the present situation came to exist. A large part of the answer undoubtedly lies in the syllabuses of our University faculties of theology. As a subject for a first degree, theology is a comparative newcomer on the scene; theology courses in this sense were introduced into English universities only in the later part of the last century, which meant that their formative period was one deeply influenced by two factors. The later nineteenth century was a period of strong denominational allegiances and of deeply felt theological differences between the denomina-

K

tions. As a result of the repeal of the Test Act those reading the new theology courses could, and did, come from a wide variety of denominations; and in the prevailing climate of opinion, that was taken to mean that the theology they contained should not be such as to trench on denominational differences. At an earlier period such a proposition might well have seemed strange, and indeed self-contradictory, meaning, as it did, that the study of theology as it was conducted in university faculties was forced to omit many of the questions which were of most immediate concern to contemporary Christians.

That such a programme was a practical possibility was due to the second of the two factors to which I referred. In the eighteenth and earlier nineteenth centuries Christianity had of course been under fairly constant attack from a number of sides. Whatever the ultimate origin and motivation of these attacks, most of them implied doubts about the Bible and so threatened the basis of all Christianity and the positions of all the denominations. These doubts were based very largely on critical and historical grounds. It was questioned, for example, whether the date and authorship of many of the biblical books were what they purported to be, whether the various books were mutually consistent and whether the events they narrated had ever occurred, or at any rate occurred as reported. Here were questions in which all denominations had a like interest, and by the latter part of the nineteenth century it was pretty generally agreed in all the major denominations that the only satisfactory way to deal with such objections was by the application of rigorous critical and historical techniques to the biblical books on the part of Christian scholars.

As understood in the later nineteenth century, history was a science, to the study of which private opinions, whether on politics or religion, or anything else, were as irrelevant as they would be to the researches of a chemist; and what was held to apply to the historical studies of biblical scholars applied equally to their archaeological, linguistic and other studies. There was thus held to be a wide area of objective study, quite vital to all Christians, in which scholars of any denomination, or none, could collaborate, not so much perhaps on an inter-denominational as on a transdenominational basis. And so far as these critical studies were concerned, there could be no objection to students of any denomination being taught by a scholar from any other.

This allegedly objective area of theological study comprised mainly biblical studies, but other aspects of Christian theology could be and were included, provided they were treated from a strictly historical point of view, and the study limited to what Christians of the past had said and done, and what they had meant by their words and deeds.

As a result of all this, higher theological education in this country assumed a more or less common pattern among all the non-Roman denominations from the time of its inception. It was generally assumed that virtually all those doing theology at universities would be candidates for orders in their various denominations; accordingly their studies were envisaged in two parts—two or three years in an interdenominational faculty, spent in studying the Bible, Church history and Christian doctrine from a strictly historical standpoint; and then a course at some theological college or seminary designed to make clear the burden of the Christian gospel in the modern world in the light of the assured results of the critical study and also of the traditions and outlook of the particular denomination concerned.

From the point of view of the university faculties this arrangement had a further advantage. From the nineteenth century onwards, university theologians have often been under fire from their secularist colleagues on the ground that their discipline is too subjective to be intellectually respectable. The division of labour I have described enabled the theologians to reply that the theological work carried on in the universities, being exclusively linguistic, historical, archaeological and so on, was as objective and scientific as the similar work done by their colleagues in other faculties. How convincing such a reply was likely to be at the time is shown, for example, by the almost rapturous terms in which Thomas Huxley, writing in 1889, described what he called 'the really scientific study of the Synoptic Gospels'. What pleased him was that theologians were studying the Gospels 'as we study fossils, to discover internal evidence of when they arose and how they came to be'. Given such a scientific approach, Huxley had, he said, no doubt that a solution was a mere question of time.[1]

It is no part of my task to defend such an arrangement on either theological or educational grounds; perhaps it was the best that could be done at the time, and certainly those who were responsible for the system were only imperfectly conscious of their motives or of the results of their arrangement. Nevertheless, some of those results are very important for our subject. One result was that when syllabuses were required for theological courses outside the universities, for example in schools and teacher training colleges, the university syllabuses naturally provided the model. Such imitation would have been natural in any case, but it was rendered inevitable by the fact that exactly the same pressures were operating on religious education outside the universities as within. Indeed the term 'Agreed Syllabus' sums up a lot of what I have been trying to say. What was not often seen, however, was that a type of course which in the universities was recognized, at least dimly, as only a preparation for theological study proper, was being treated elsewhere as 'religious studies' full stop. For the school children or teacher trainees who were put through such courses —or even for the increasing number of non-ordinands reading theology at the universities, often with a view to teaching— there was in most cases to be no equivalent for the ordinand's further study at theological college or seminary.

To some extent that was recognized but regarded as unavoidable in a state system of education; but a number of factors combined to obscure its full significance. In many of the most influential schools and colleges it was still possible to supple-

[1] *Science and Christian Tradition*, page 270. Quoted by W. R. Farmer in *The Synoptic Problem*, page 180.

ment this type of theological study either with overt denominational instruction or with the teaching of a sort of generalized dogmatic Christianity.

Second, and perhaps more important, it must be remembered that the period I have been discussing was the heyday of theological liberalism. For our purposes the important thing about theological liberalism is its distrust of elaborate theological constructions, indeed of theological construction of any kind, and its belief that it was precisely critical study of the Bible and Christian doctrine which, if carried through with sufficient rigour, would yield the true theology. In Harnack's *What Is Christianity?*, for example, first published in 1900, it is argued that the way to discover the true Christianity is not by any process of construction or theologizing, but precisely by using critical scholarship to peel the onion, as it were, clear away all past theological constructions—even St Paul's—and get back to the simple religion of Jesus, which concerned not his own status and person, but the fatherhood of God and the brotherhood of man. On such a view—and this book is very typical of its period—critical biblical study *needs* no supplementing; by itself it uncovers the true religion in a form more or less immediately acceptable to contemporary western man. It may be true, as Dr Vidler has recently argued, that this generally accepted interpretation of Harnack in fact does him something of an injustice, but it was generally accepted during the period I am discussing, and the impact of theological liberalism in the schools was all the greater because it was believed that the essential Christianity which it discloses is particularly well suited to the needs, outlook and comprehension of children. I can myself remember how constantly in school services during the late twenties and early thirties we worked through a small selection of hymns from *Songs of Praise* which reflected such a liberal theology.

O Son of Man, our hero strong and tender,
Whose servants are the brave in all the earth. . . .

It is probably true that theological liberalism remained the dominant influence in the schools much longer than it did among professional theologians. However, and this is the third point I want to make in this connexion, where it did begin to be superseded after the first war, the movements which succeeded it, particularly the so-called 'crisis theology' or biblical theology, while they were utterly opposed to its procedure and *simpliste* conclusions, themselves had characteristics which tended to mask our problem. To some extent they could be interpreted as a return to the traditional Protestant doctrinal position and so give the impression that the earlier emphasis on biblical criticism has been excessive and that nothing much was required for divinity teaching beyond a general grounding in the traditional Christian position. So far as teachers came under the influence of these movements they often tended, it is true, to feel frustrated by the almost exclusively biblical emphasis in school syllabuses, but this was largely offset by another characteristic of the post-liberal movements, what I might call their near fundamentalism.

After the first war a good deal of the interest in biblical studies shifted from historial criticism to linguistic criticism and philological research. This was the era of Kittel's *Wörterbuch* and Sir Edwyn Hoskyns. Every effort was made to discover the precise meaning of the terms used in the Bible and early Christian literature, and as a result much work of lasting value was done and, I should add, is still being done; but the assumption behind this work generally was that once the original meaning of the terms was revealed, the theologian's task was largely done. There would emerge from the Bible a series of genuinely historical events which modern man could interpret and accept, very much as the biblical writers—and, it may be added, traditional orthodoxy—had done, as an interrelated series of divine interventions in history which had in principle achieved the world's salvation and only awaited the full working out of their consequences.

Once again, on such a view, biblical studies required comparatively little supplementation; and I suspect that the influence of this sort of position has combined with the wide resurgence of a cruder type of fundamentalism to produce a situation in which far too much of the divinity teaching in our schools is fundamentalist, at any rate in its general implications and in the impact it makes on the pupils. Deeply though I deplore this, I do not fail to appreciate the motives which often lie behind it. Conscientious teachers who want to make religious instruction live up to its name, but are largely limited by the syllabuses to a study of a biblical text on a non-denominational basis, are naturally tempted to go for the religion in the only place in the situation where they can find any, in the religious ideas of the text as they stand. The best exponents of biblical theology would regard the sort of thing I have in mind as a travesty of their position, but their movement has undoubtedly been influential in giving such a procedure a certain air of intellectual respectability. Indeed the position of the conscientious teacher who does not want to follow such a procedure is not altogether an enviable one. He has an uneasy feeling that the older liberal approach has been discredited, and what he has seen of the 'new theologians' on the television does not perhaps suggest that they have much positive help to give him; small wonder then if he falls back on sincerity, commonsense and experience of life as being the only qualifications for divinity teaching; and on the basis of them seeks to inject what illumination he can into that 'exchange of mutual mystification' which is so often the free discussion, or religious instruction, period.

Such a reaction is, as I have said, quite understandable, and it is all the easier because a belief that sincerity and conviction are the sole qualifications necessary for divinity teaching has long been almost an article of faith in some educational circles. But however deeply ingrained, or understandable, such a belief may be, it is, I believe, totally mistaken. Whatever else the theological movements of the last forty-five years may have done, they have surely put it beyond doubt that Christianity is an interpretation of life and a response to life which are quite specific because they are specifically related to certain past events and certain interpretations of them. If they are to be so much as explained—I do not say communicated—to others, they must, like any other subject-matter, first be learned.

But what are this interpretation of life and this response to life? Can theologians or anyone else offer any unified account of them, and, even if they can, have we any right, in an 'open' society, to put before our children one particular interpretation of things? Let us take these questions in order.

The situation in contemporary theology is certainly kaleidoscopic. In the last twenty years or so, and even more within the last ten years, and even the last five years, things have developed with almost unbelievable rapidity, and it would be idle to pretend that theology speaks today with anything like a single voice. One point of great importance should be made, however. The differences between theologians are no longer due, to anything like the extent they were, to denominational *parti pris*. To a great extent they cut across denominational boundaries—even the boundary between the Roman Catholics and the rest—and seem increasingly to be due to genuinely *academic* disagreements about the meaning of evidence and the like, such as occur in all intellectual disciplines. This is surely a fact of great importance in relation to religious education in the schools.

What is the present position in theology? Obviously I have neither the competence, nor the time now, to take you on a conducted tour of contemporary theological scholarship, but if I have to try and sum the position up, I should say that what has happened is that the 'new' movement of thought in Europe which began, according to Bonhoeffer, in the thirteenth century and passed on through the renaissance to gain such immense momentum in the last two centuries, has begun to make its full impact on English theological thinking. English theologians were slow to recognize the major cultural revolution which, as C. S. Lewis and others have shown, has occurred in the western world since about the middle of the eighteenth century; but they are recognizing it now and are acutely—some would say almost morbidly—conscious that the cultural context in which they are working is *toto coelo* different from that in which the New Testament was written and the classical creeds were formulated.

And this recognition has brought home to them the fact that any statement in words, however true, is always relative to the cultural context in which it is made. It presupposes a whole host of assumptions on a wide variety of matters, and insofar as these assumptions get changed, any truth in the original statement needs to be stated in quite new ways if it is to be either intelligible or acceptable. This question of *restatement* is, in various guises, a major preoccupation with most theologians today. Significantly, the most quoted words in contemporary English theological discussion are probably two statements by Dr Leonard Hodgson to the effect that to say 'the Bible says . . .' gets nowhere; the question we have to ask is: 'What must the truth be, and have been, if people who thought as they did put it like that?'[1]

Before I follow that up, however, there is another aspect of the situation to be mentioned. One consequence of the modern cultural revolution has been the recognition that history is not the objective study the Victorians imagined. How you interpret historical evidence will depend quite largely on your presuppositions, and what you take to be the meaning of a historical document will depend on the questions—implicit and explicit —with which you come to the study of it. The importance and inescapability of subjectivity is something the modern theologian has had to learn together with his colleagues in history, natural science and other disciplines.

On the basis of a new understanding of history and allied disciplines, theologians are re-examining many of the

[1] *For Faith and Freedom.*
   ii p. 12. Blackwell 1957 and i p. 88. Blackwell 1956.

supposedly 'assured results' of earlier scholars and finding them anything but 'assured'. The Pentateuchal sources J, D, P and E long ago went into the melting pot; the existence of Q has come in for considerable doubt, and recently a book has appeared by a reputable American scholar seriously questioning the priority of Mark's Gospel. So far as St Paul is concerned, there have been the interesting, if not so far entirely convincing, attempts to demonstrate the inauthenticity of most of his epistles, by methods which involve the use of a computer. Of more obviously immediate interest, and also more soundly based, is the work being done by a group of German theologians on the question of the historical Jesus. They have come to doubt both the optimism of the liberals with regard to the quest of the historical Jesus, and the equally extreme pessimism of certain more recent scholarship, and they are hopeful that by the use of certain new methods, rigorously applied, they may be able to give us, not indeed a life of Jesus, but a reasonably firmly based account of his self-understanding and the major claims and demands he made. And they believe they can show that the claims made for Jesus by later Christians, while not identical with the claims he made himself, were to a considerable extent legitimate re-statements of them for the situations in which they were made.

There is much in this and similar work that would make exciting hearing in the appropriate forms of schools, not least because no claims are made for 'assured results', but there is an exhilarating sense of real discovery and of openness to see what conclusions will emerge. Moreover I do not believe anyone could learn about such work without being impressed by the sheer acuteness with which it is being carried on and the determination to follow strictly scientific methods, often in contexts where such methods are hard to devise.

That leads me to insert a parenthesis. I have an impression that a good deal of sixth form discussion is dominated by a suspicion that Christian thinkers are less able, and indeed less honest, intellectually, than those who disagree with them.

It is somehow always 'doubt' which is 'honest', and being a genuine intellectual more or less implies agnosticism. Such a suspicion, if it exists, seems to me unfortunate for the simple reason that I do not believe it is justified. I am not sure how it arose, but the best way to dispel it is surely to familiarize sixth formers with some of the work that is currently going on in theology. To put it crudely, no schoolboy who knew anything of the work of a Bultmann, a Tillich, a de Chardin or a Marcel could suppose that their minds were appreciably less able or their methods less intellectually respectable than those, let us say, of a Russell, a Sartre, a Hoyle or an A. J. P. Taylor.

The critical and historical work to which I have referred is all connected with the Bible, but equally interesting work is being done in connexion with the history and thought of the Church, and much of it is very important. Nevertheless, as I implied earlier, such work is not the only, or even probably the chief, centre of interest in contemporary theology. The issues between theologians which make the headlines are not, as they once were, questions about the interpretation or authenticity of parts of the Bible, but questions about how the Christian faith must be stated in our time, about what beliefs it commits us to and what conduct it entails. Whatever may be thought of Bishop Robinson's recent books, in the type of question with which they are concerned they undoubtedly reflect a prevailing trend in modern theology.

'What must the truth be if men who thought as the biblical and early Christian writers did, put it like that?' So posed, the question would seem to expect an answer in two stages. First let the critical and historical theologians tell us what the gospel meant in the cultural context of the early centuries, and then, as a second stage, we will find the terms in which to express the same meaning for ourselves and our contemporaries. No doubt some part of the truth lies along these lines, but the matter is more complex. You cannot so easily separate what the gospel *meant* from what it *means*. At the risk of over-simplifying wildly, may I try to say something briefly about the process of reorientation which has been taking place in recent theology with such marked results? If it will no longer do just to say 'The Bible says . . .' or 'the creeds say . . .', how are we to treat the words of the Bible and other authoritative Christian literature? You might put it that we have to discover from them what being a Christian really meant for those who wrote them, in order that we may see what it 'really means' to be a Christian in the changed circumstances of our time. However, the question what it 'really meant' for St Paul, or St Athanasius, or Luther to be a Christian is a deceptively simple one.

To begin with, we depend for an answer mainly on written sources, and writing is normally done at the conceptual level. Yet it is increasingly recognized that religion is something which touches men at many levels beside the conceptual. The student of Christian literature must therefore have the sensitivity to distinguish in his documents what is to be taken at its conceptual face-value and what is to be interpreted as 'myth', shall we say—that is, as the conceptualization, or even the rationalization, of things really different and sometimes deeper. Which raises of course the further question what that something different or deeper is.

That launches us on yet a further set of questions; for if we ask what it 'really' meant for St Paul to be a Christian, the word 'really' implies a criterion which is derived as much from *our* experience and concerns as from St Paul's. At least part of the meaning of our question is: what was there in St Paul's experience of being a Christian which answers to our experience or speaks to our condition in the twentieth century?

Here is a problem. How far is it a valid procedure to decide in the light of our experiences, needs and cultural context what is of 'real', or central, significance in St Paul's statements? On this theologians are by no means entirely agreed; and even if, with the majority, we regard such a procedure as at least partly legitimate, and indeed unavoidable, we have still to ask what are the aspects and areas of twentieth century life against the background of which we must read St Paul's epistles if they are to yield their message in a form that we can cope with. We have seen that what a text yields depends on the questions with which we approach it; what are the modern questions with which we must approach St Paul's epistles if they are to disclose their relevance—assuming they have any relevance—to our circumstances?

Here there is nothing like a consensus of opinion among theologians. There are even some—I think, for example, of Paul van Buren's recent book[1]—who seem to think that none of the questions involved need presuppose belief in any super-natural being or transcendent realm. The great majority of theologians at present would hotly dispute that, but they would agree with van Buren to the extent of thinking that the questions should all be such as have implications for our self-under-standing and our practical response to life. There are few theologians now who hold that the Bible is meant to answer cosmological or biological questions, or even, to more than a limited degree, historical or strictly metaphysical questions.

The problem remains, however, of discovering what questions it *is* legitimate to put to the Bible. If the Bible and other Christian writing are worth study at all, that is presumably because they contain things pertinent to our situation and our predicament. What then *are* our situation and predicament? No doubt we all have our own ideas. There is the problem of identity, for example. Who am I and how did I become what I am? There is the social problem. How is it that man appears to be by nature a political animal and yet his social relations at all levels are so universally bedevilled? Then there are the problems on the border between psychology and metaphysics. How should I respond to my environment and where can I get the power to do so? Is reality hostile to me or can I believe that I am accepted? As I say, we should all have candidate questions, but it will not do to single out questions haphazardly

[1] *The Secular Meaning of the Gospel.* (S.C.M. Press, 1963).

and unsystematically, and theologians are undoubtedly determined to take very seriously this matter of discovering the right questions to ask. In the effort to discover them various theologians are familiarizing themselves with the work of different non-theologians in almost every field.

There are, for example, the profound phenomenological analyses of the human situation made by such existentialist thinkers as Martin Heidegger. These have been heavily drawn on by theologians like Rudolf Bultmann and Paul Tillich. Others, Mr Harry Williams, for example, have looked to the work of novelists and also of psychoanalysts. At a more conceptual level, others have grappled with modern philosophy, particularly in the empiricist and linguistic analyst schools. Others again—and I think particularly of the American theologian Reinhold Niebuhr—have looked to the sociologists and anthropologists and their various analyses of man's social situation. Another example would be Teilhard de Chardin with his expert 'inside' knowledge of the biological and palaeontological realms, or there is the work of Professor Smart and others who are trying to enter into genuine and detailed dialogue with adherents of other religions in the hope of learning from them some of the questions we must ask.

Needless to say, none of these approaches regards itself as *the* right one, to the exclusion of the others. The overall picture is one of search and desire to learn. 'The mood,' it has been said, 'is one of *exploration* rather than *explanation*,'[1] and theology, with what we may well regard as befitting modesty, is perhaps ready to see itself more in the role of midwife than of queen.

As a result, contemporary theologians can easily appear to be quite without a clue, going round cap in hand to all their secular colleagues in turn, in the hope of discovering from them answers which they cannot produce themselves. That is the sort of impression that appears to have been given by certain

[1] Canon S. H. Evans, Dean of King's College, London.

television broadcasts, at any rate to those determined to interpret them in that way. But such an interpretation is, I believe,
to a large extent a false one. Theologians have a shrewder idea
what they are doing than they are sometimes given credit for.
They are concerned to discover the genuine questions to which
our situation gives rise in the belief that if they approach the
Bible and the Christian tradition with them, the confrontation
will be a creative one from which truth—they might even dare
to say, in a sense, *the* truth—about our situation will emerge.
The proof of the pudding is in the eating and I suggest that
anyone who has read, for example, Mr Harry Williams' recent
volume of sermons, which comes out of an equally profound
knowledge of modern novels, modern psychoanalysis and the
Christian tradition, will not want lightly to dismiss such an
approach. Or there are the various works of Reinhold Niebuhr
in which his close and deep study of the contemporary social
situation has enabled him to win considerable illumination on
it from the Bible and the Christian tradition. Many more examples could be cited, and in fact the risk I have run by putting
things as I have is that I may have unduly exaggerated the
tentative and exploratory character of modern theology and
the degree of discontinuity between the work of contemporary
theologians and that of their predecessors, from the biblical
writers onwards. Over the generations theology has in fact
built up a considerable amount of know-how, particularly on
the side of methodology, and it can fairly claim to be an independent academic discipline comprising many different
elements which it has some idea how to organize in a rational
hierarchy and to relate on sound methodological principles. I
myself tried to say something about that in an inaugural lecture
given here six or seven years ago; and though I should now
want to express myself rather differently, I think it was the
details of my description which may have been wrong, and
not the claim for theology as a many-sided but integrated
discipline, in which significant work is being done both in
the various specialist departments and at the level of attempts

at synthesis. In particular, in the matter of presenting the gospel in a way relevant to the understanding and needs of today, slow but solid advance has undoubtedly been made in the last thirty or forty years, largely perhaps because it has been possible to draw on the earlier work of such men as Schleiermacher and Wilhelm Dilthey, who in their turn could build on work which has been going on in Germany at least since the Reformation.

The upshot of all this is certainly rather perplexing. On the one hand, theology is probably less dogmatic today than it has ever been in the past. Theologians are very much alive to the possible inadequacies and admixture of error in their formulations; and they certainly have no wish to claim them as irreformable and timelessly valid statements of the truth; they realize now that no statements in human words can ever be that. Nonetheless they are convinced that in 'the things concerning Jesus' and even somewhere in the area of what they say about them, lies the clue to the true understanding of reality and the right response to it. 'How to be tentative in theology while being sure in religion'—that is Professor I. T. Ramsey's formulation of the theologian's problem and it contains an important clue. Theologians are almost all people of religious convictions, and the faith and experience which underlie those convictions leave them in no doubt that certain things must be said, even if, paradoxically, they are not absolutely clear what those things are or how to say them. They sometimes disagree fairly sharply on the question how far the things that are being said and have been said in the Church are adequate to what must be said, but there it is important to avoid a misunderstanding. The fact that a man is highly critical of the adequacy of what is being said implies no lack of conviction on his part about 'the things concerning Jesus' and the need to proclaim and interpret them. That should be borne in mind in discussing the Bishop of Woolwich, for example. In any case I think all theologians would agree that so far as school children are concerned, there are things which ought to be said to them, and at that level can be said, things so vital that not to be exposed to them would be a serious deprivation.

In this regard we are apt, I think, to be misled sometimes by the complexity and technicality of much modern theology. For instance, the debate about the presentation of the New Testament gospel in current terms, particularly on its 'demythologization' side, is being carried on in a jargon which is increasingly technical to a frankly terrifying degree. Nonetheless I believe a competent teacher could explain both the basic problems and the main lines of solution to children in the upper forms of schools in a way which they would find both illuminating and exciting, and which might incidentally set Bible reading in a quite new perspective for them as a live option.

In connexion with the whole question of teaching theology in schools I should like, in conclusion, to make four points.

First, if there is any truth in the picture I have been giving you, theologians today are not liable to the charge which sixth-formers have so often brought against them, the charge of having the ivory tower mentality, of discussing abstract metaphysical questions with no practical relevance for themselves or anyone else. One of the main tendencies in modern theology is to insist that theological statements can only be meaningful if they have some existential implications, if there are some conditions in experience by which they can be verified or falsified. And there is no need to give further publicity to the efforts of Canon Rhymes and those who think like him— and indeed those who do not—to draw out the moral implications of Christianity in the sexual sphere, the economic sphere and many other practical spheres which are of very immediate concern to those in the upper forms of schools.

Secondly, I spoke quite deliberately of teaching *theology* in the schools because I believe that is what you have got to do; or shall I put it that the words "religious instruction" have got to mean what they say? I tried to show at the beginning of this

L

lecture that the reasons which led people to think otherwise were peculiar to a particular epoch and that the attempted limitation of religious instruction to biblical and critical studies was never really satisfactory. In the University theological faculties today, although the old division of labour still largely persists, one hears increasing criticism of it and syllabus revision designed to make the degrees genuinely *theological* degrees is almost everywhere under consideration; though it is only fair to add that there are strong objectors, and indeed genuine difficulties, to it. Still, if the teaching in the schools is to reflect the genuine insights of contemporary theology, it must go beyond the limits of critical biblical and historical studies and try to show what religious insights arise from them. Such a programme is obviously not without difficulties in a situation where people are by no means entirely agreed what religious insights *do* emerge. However, as I have said, the disagreements between denominations and theologians are by no means as great or important as is sometimes supposed; and where they do occur, I see no reason to doubt that children are quite capable of appreciating the principles and issues involved and that they would find the discussion of them rewarding and stimulating. The great thing is to show them how the various views of denominations and individuals are so many attempts to draw out the meaning of the original revelation, as critically studied, and to explain the principles on which they can decide responsibly between them, now and in later life. If that seems to lack the note of ecclesiastical authority associated with religious teaching in all the denominations, it must be borne in mind that religious instruction in the schools of an 'open' society rightly differs in certain respects from religious instruction as given to the children of committed believers within the context of a particular denomination. But in all the religious teaching given to senior schoolchildren I should want to lay quite considerable stress on opening up to the pupils the ways in which religious truth is arrived at and derived from the sources, and on encouraging them to discuss the matter so far as they are able. Given the situation in theology I have described, and the varieties in current theological thinking, such a method of religious instruction, at any rate for the more advanced pupils, seems to me the most defensible, on educational grounds, and, as I shall try to show in a moment, on other grounds as well.

My third point follows from the last, and from a good deal else that I have been saying, so obviously that it needs little elaboration. For the sort of divinity teaching I have in mind we need teachers who are as much trained specialists as their colleagues in other subjects. They need to know about modern critical studies and to be at home in the current theological debate in a way that presupposes at least a specialist diploma course and preferably some study of theology at degree level. Indeed one of the strongest reasons for wanting to alter the pattern of theology teaching in the Universities and to have more composite degrees which include theology is in order to be able to make better provision for would-be divinity teachers. It is very satisfactory that several of the theology faculties in the modern Universities are striking out in new directions with the current theological situation and the needs of would-be teachers very much in mind.

In my last point I must try to grasp a nettle. I have been arguing for a type of divinity teaching which, so far as is possible in view of current denominational and theological disagreements, would put before children the specifically Christian interpretation of, and response to, reality. It would be genuine religious instruction, though of course it would be given in a reasoned way which tried to show on what facts the Christian faith is based and how it claims to be derived from them. The latter could hardly be made intelligible without something being said about the interpretative authority claimed, in some form or other, by all branches of the Church, and also about the past and present religious experience to which the Christian faith appeals at many points.

Would such a form of religious instruction be legitimate in state schools? So far as the (non-Roman) denominations are concerned, I should be very surprised if there were any objections from them to the sort of thing I have in mind. The question would rather be one about the legitimacy of using taxpayers' money in this way.

On such a question I can obviously claim no special competence to speak, though it is naturally one to which I have given some thought, if only because the same sort of question can fairly be raised about theological faculties in the Universities, in view of the present tendency for their work to become more specifically theological. For what it is worth, my view on the facts and the rights of the matter is something like this.

Everyone, I think, would agree about the need for all of us, including the children, to achieve some perspective on the various aspects and activities of life, from which they make some sense and have some meaning. Certainly we need some view of life such as may provide a basis for moral judgements and motivation for moral conduct. Most people, I think, even most non-Christians, would go further and agree that the Christian claim to provide such a view and perspective, and the motive power to live accordingly, is too venerable and well supported to be lightly discarded. There are few who want to suppress all theology and theologians and would not want Christianity to be given the opportunity to develop its position and claims as fully and cogently as possible. Indeed in many of the public and private comments that followed the publication of *Honest to God*, I think I detected a certain note of pleased surprise. People seemed to be saying: 'If theologians are addressing themselves to the sort of issues canvassed in this book, instead of being largely preoccupied, as we had supposed, with purely antiquarian problems, we are certainly disposed to listen carefully to what they have to say.' The feeling seemed to be: 'If we are going to have theologians, let them do genuine theology; let them work out what the Christian position involves today, in terms both of belief and practice, and present it to us in such a way that we may be able to make a responsible judgement upon it.'

If there is any truth in this, its bearing on our topic will be obvious enough. There are few parents, I believe, who would not want their children presented with a clear account, appropriate to their level, of the Christian position in faith and morals as drawn by the best modern exponents from the Bible and the tradition. Of course it would be presented for free discussion and in full confrontation with other positions, equally freely presented; but the discussion that followed would be informed discussion, such as is only possible on the basis of expert instruction. As things are at present in the western world, everyone is bound sooner or later to be brought into contact with Christianity in one connexion or another. Is it not best—to put the matter on the lowest plane—that they should have a reasonably accurate idea what it is they are dealing with?

CHAPTER X

THE STANDPOINT OF THE SECULAR HUMANIST

LIONEL ELVIN

May I first comment on three terms, none of which is quite clear by itself, but which it will be convenient to adopt in practice? First, religious education. This is really a very wide term, but when I use it in this paper I shall refer to what passes under that name, or the name of religious instruction (chiefly of course with reference to the Christian religion) in this country. Secondly, when I refer to schools, I mean not all schools, but those that are fully maintained by public funds and belong to public authorities. Thirdly, secular humanist. Humanist, by itself, is now used to describe those who do not invoke the concept of the supernatural in their account of man and the universe. But it has been used more widely, and some Christians feel that the term Christian humanist has historical warrant, as is indeed so. Though the term secular humanist is also not altogether satisfactory, it will be simplest to adopt it for the present paper instead of the word humanist by itself for the sense described above.

Now if you ask a person what he thinks about religious education in schools he will commonly reply by telling you what his own religious beliefs, or lack of them, may be. This is not entirely to misconstrue the question. If we were all of one religion in this country, or all immune to it, we should want the schools in what they inculcated to follow the completely accepted pattern of society; and since we no doubt all wish everybody did share our views (whatever they may be) to explain what those views are may not be ultimately irrelevant. But the question is largely misconstrued if this kind of answer is given; for we are not all of one mind in these matters. Yet we do make up one national society, and the schools are the schools of all of us. We must start therefore with the fact that although we have a common system of schools we are a very mixed and differentiated society in our views on and about religion. It follows therefore that the ground of our discussion is in the first place not that of religion as such, but of social policy, indeed of decisions that must be made through politics.

That we are so mixed a society that we cannot be described simply as either Christian or non-Christian seems to be generally agreed. Indeed, Professor Niblett, writing as a Christian, went so far as to call one of his books *Christian Education in a Secular Society*. Most people would agree that we have a sizeable minority of practising Christians with active beliefs and smaller religious minorities of some size in particular schools (not only our traditional Jewish community but Hindus, Sikhs and Muslims also). Then at the other end of the spectrum we have those parents who quite consciously (whether organized or not—and most of them are not) do not accept any religious position, the secular humanists and near-humanists. In between we have the very large middle group of people, perhaps not very analytical or reflective about these matters, who hardly ever go to church, and who feel no reason to go there to express any religious beliefs, but who tend to use the churches for the ritual purposes of weddings and funerals. If you asked these if they believed in a God, many would say 'I suppose so, in a kind of way'; others would say 'Well, I don't really know that I do very much'. While if you pointed the question a little more and asked if they believed in a loving personal God and his son Jesus Christ who has saved us all, most would be a little embarrassed and say 'Well, that's what the parson says, and I don't say he's wrong, and I suppose I believe it in a way, but that sort of thing doesn't mean a great deal to me.' Convinced Christians, no doubt, would like to see this middle group's attitude not as one of negative indifference but of passive acceptance; while secular humanists would say that the general trend of the times will make the idea of a God seem still more distant to these people or their children, so that in terms of their behaviour they will probably become clearly agnostic. At any rate, that we are mixed in some way as this I think no one will seriously dispute.

Now if we are such a multi-belief society, this raises an immediate question as to equality of treatment among different groups of citizens, and in particular equality of treatment in the schools. Our original question, with its inadequate answer, then becomes a differently formulated question, to wit: 'On what grounds can you claim that you have a right to inculcate your opinions on a controversial matter through the common schools, while those who with equal right hold views different from yours are denied that opportunity?' *The Times* (April 29, 1965) notes that of 359 people questioned by Mr Geoffrey Gorer only eleven held orthodox beliefs on an after life, and a quarter stated firmly that they did not believe in a future after death. Why should the eleven have a monopoly of official expression in our common society's schools?

It is sometimes said that hardly anyone will object to a fair and tolerant presentation of Christianity in the schools. It is true that some parents with no beliefs of their own tolerate this, feeling it does no particular harm, but others (and it will be an increasing number, as Mr Harold Pinter observed in his recent protest about it) feel extremely annoyed that their children should have inculcated into them beliefs for which they see no foundation and which they themselves actively reject. To take a quite central example. The affirmation of the Resurrection is that a man who was in a unique sense human and divine lived on the earth, was crucified and died, and after three days rose from the dead. Many people now, and not only active secular humanists, feel that this is a pretty improbable story. Children in the common schools are taught that this happened—and by happened I mean happened. Those who believe it have every right to their belief; but so do those who do not. Why should our common schools give every opportunity to inculcate their belief to those who say it did happen, and give no such opportunity to those who do not think it a reasonable thing to believe? If our schools engaged in militant propaganda for atheism there would be an outcry from Christian believers, and properly so. The latter, however, find it difficult to understand that humanist parents may suffer a similar offence, from the same situation in reverse.

Let us see now how this affects the teachers. Christian observers have commented on the fact that not all teachers seem to enter into the act of worship every morning with much sense of conviction and that the attitude to the religious education period is sometimes one of 'Well, we've been saddled with this period, so now what can we do with it? But of course, what else can be expected? If you have a society in which only a minority consists of active practising Christians, how can you expect a corps of teachers virtually all of whom are active, practising Christians? Such are the pressures on schoolteachers to be conventional that probably the incidence of religious belief is somewhat higher among them than among the general public, just as the incidence among university teachers is probably somewhat lower. Many Christians have not agreed in their hearts that a man or woman can be just as good a teacher, and should have fully equal rights in our common schools, whether he is a practising Christian or not. So we have pressures that inevitably induce semi-hypocrisy in the profession that above all should be committed to intellectual honesty.

It may be argued that such teachers are really very few in number, and there is in any case a conscience clause that enables them not to take part. There is strong reason to suppose that the number of those who are either secular humanists outright, or who are doubtful enough not to wish to make public witness of things of which they are far from sure, is much larger than the religious suppose. This is for two reasons, one understandable if not laudable, the other altogether laudable. The first reason is that although a candidate for a headship may not be asked a direct question about religious beliefs it is quite obvious that the head of a school who does not wish to conduct a service of worship places others as well as himself in an awkward position. And apart from promotion, a teacher who abstains from what is officially a school activity is of less than full value to a school and is likely to be thought of as awkward and unco-operative. So, knowing this perfectly well, many teachers find discretion the better part of valour.

The second reason is that secular humanists, are on the whole a modest and unargumentative lot. This statement may surprise people who carry an image of the nineteenth century secularist in mind, the kind of secularist who was a religious sectarian turned upside down. That is not the kind of secular humanist one meets now. He knows that his secular humanism is negative. Indeed, I have never understood why people should think it a telling criticism that secular humanism is negative. If you are asked whether you think a belief in supernatural beings well founded, and say no, of course your position is negative. Grammar alone makes it so. But it doesn't mean that your life is negative, and you certainly do not want to spend all your time saying 'no'. You want to get on with the positive interests and activities of your life. So although a few humanists, with a feeling for the principles at stake, join an appropriate society, most of them just come to their own conclusions and leave it at that. So, for both these reasons, people like myself have a distinct feeling that we are speaking for more teachers and educationists than those the Christian 'Establishment' suppose to exist.

It should not call for much analytical power to distinguish between expressing an opinion as to what one thinks is right and implying that one's own view is the only one that can be thought right, yet this distinction seems beyond many of those who advocate religious education in schools. Such people may not realize that this is insulting to those who disagree with them and have just as much claim to have their views respected.

I have been looking at a publication of the Institute of Christian Education issued in 1964, 'Religious Education in the Nursery and Infant Schools'. On page thirty-nine it discusses the compulsory morning 'act of worship', and it says about it—'It is imperative that this act of worship be planned and conducted carefully and with conviction, and that it be regarded by all as of overriding importance in the life of the school, because the quality of that life is profoundly influenced by it. Above all, the impression must be avoided that the service is a mere minor appendage to a routine assembly of the whole school. The important thing to remember is that every school assembly is an avenue for the activity of God'. This is indeed mandatory. It commands teachers that they must believe something! The act of worship, too, must be so regarded *by all*. Now if the writers had said—'We think the best kind of school is a Christian school, in which all the children and teachers are Christians and come together every morning to worship the God in whom they believe', one might or might not share that view, but could take no civic objection to the statement. But to insist that all teachers and all parents and children in a mixed society must share and express the same beliefs is not only to live in an unreal world but to be quite intolerant. It is further insulting, because it implies that those teachers who do not wish to be active participants in such a public service have less than a real right in the school. Yet these schools are the schools of our whole, mixed society. Modest and patient as we humanists are, we find this not acceptable at all. The schools of this most diverse society are not to be the exclusive preserve of a sect or any combination of sects. They belong to the British public, most of whom never think of going to church on a Sunday. This attitude towards teachers in our schools is quite different, moreover, from anything one finds in the universities, where the opinions of teachers as to religion and their decision to enter into or refrain from activities associated with religion are entirely their own business. Any one who works in a University Institute of Education, in contact with both worlds, is made very conscious of this difference. There can surely be no disagreement as to which official attitude is proper.

On page twenty-three this same publication notes that for some children prayers at schools will follow on naturally from prayers at home (a very small proportion, one might surmise) though for others it will be an experience that will be confined to school life; and it adds: 'It is the sincerity and integrity of the teacher that will surmount this hurdle'. But suppose that the sincerity and integrity of the teacher impel him *not* to engage in such exercises? Are sincerity and integrity only to be respected in believers? Let me repeat that it is absurd to expect that from a general population of great diversity of views about religion there will emerge a corps of teachers every one of whom will wish to be known as a zealous and practising Christian. This is a fact that the advocates of the compulsory 'act of worship' simply must face. A young teacher wrote about this in the organ of the National Union of Teachers (*The Teacher*, February 28, 1964), He said:

> Such an assembly necessitates some reverence, even if only simulated. The enforced quiet is the responsibility of the adult teachers sprinkled among the children, waiting for the entry of the officers each morning.
>
> What worries me is that I am required to do this every morning in defiance of any conscience I might have. Maybe it is because I am new that I chafe at the hypocrisy required of me. I must police children and mumble hymns and prayers, without believing at all in either the ceremony itself or the wider implications of it. Nobody seems to care that there is any hypocrisy.

He says that of course you may contract out, but if you raise the question you are put off with talk about the value of assemblies and it is assumed that, like playground duty, this is one of the things all the staff should do. He asks in how many schools this freedom to contract out has any substance. 'And,' he adds, 'we have our references to think of.'

Those who wish to retain the religious clauses of the 1944 Act have the moral responsibility for this state of affairs. I do not think that they can defend it.

With this publication of the Institute of Christian Education in front of me I pass on to observe that much of the material proffering guidance to teachers about religious education is at a very primitive intellectual level, which increases the offensiveness of the compulsion behind it. I do not of course mean that abstract concepts should be presented to young children or should form the basis of their teaching. I am saying that teachers of such children should not be presented with arguments that are patently bogus. Thus, this publication (on page nine) gives a short account of the stages of emotional growth of children, and ends: 'Finally, with the development of self-discipline learnt through mutual respect and love comes the realization that it is not only necessary, but good and right to obey the laws of God.' Now as a statement either of biological development or of social development as such this is not true. It is true only of children in whose society or family children have been led to think so. What happens if you indoctrinate children in a certain way cannot honestly be smuggled in to what purports to be an account of growth as such. Incidentally, it is of some interest to note that the publication speaks of seeing that it is right to obey the laws of God. This is a very different statement from saying that it is right to do good because that is pleasing to God. The first is authoritarian and permits of no compromise with the secular humanist—indeed, with the humanist of any kind. The second does permit much agreement in practice, because it assumes that we can, as men and women, discuss what it is good and not good to do.

Again, this publication illustrates a common tendency in such intellectually slack circles to describe anything generally felt to be good as really 'religious'. I quote—'It is surely the aim of a truly religious education to ensure that young children are nurtured in such a way that life speaks to them of love and accompanying trust, of beauty with its attendant wonder, of freedom with its necessary responsibility, of joy with an underlying gaiety.'—How is this 'religious' education? It might pass for a general description of our aims in bringing up children, though in terms of a too easy lyricism that we should not perhaps permit ourselves in our own lectures on education to intending teachers. If this serves as an account of truly religious education, why have a religious education period at all? It is done all the time, throughout the school, anyway.

On page thirteen we are told—'The child who has seen the emerging wonder of a daffodil planted deep in the dark earth—a dry, lifeless looking thing—now triumphantly bursting with bright colour in the springtime has learned more of wonder, of life and resurrection, than the child who is told "God makes the pretty flowers".' Now the key word here—the sleight-of-hand word—is of course 'resurrection'. One realizes this when later (on page twenty-six) there is a list of things that should be taught in the class. These include the resurrection, but of course this time *the* Resurrection, that is to say of Jesus. The way has been prepared. Now to suggest that there is a parallel here, that because daffodils come up in the spring we must believe the resurrection story is not treating children, let alone their teachers, with respect. The flowers that bloom in the spring have nothing to do with the case. Are we still at the stage of Mrs Gatty's *Parables from Nature?* I am sorry if my bluntness offends any one. But if we say that this sort of thing is just not respectable the fault is not ours. When we complain about the lack of intellectual respectability of much that passes for religious education we are of course not impugning university scholars whose honesty and rigour no one doubts at all. We are talking of what actually is recommended, and no doubt goes on, in schools. I do not think such looseness would appear in recommendations to teachers for any other subject in our schools.

It would be tempting to go on, if only to comment on the

story of the little girl who tried to telephone Jesus to thank him for the recovery of her mother from illness (which is praised as truly praying), and to comment on it in the light of a sermon I once heard by Dean Inge in the University Church at Cambridge—after the Bidding Prayer had been said, of course—pointing out the foolishness of petitionary prayer. But enough. Let me now make two general observations.

First, of course, one speaks simply to young children. But in all other subjects we try to do so in such a way that they will not positively have to unlearn what we teach them when young. And if we 'speak in parables' we try to do so in parables that do not induce bad mental habits and that do in a broad way fit. Incidentally, why has the parable of the Good Samaritan had such a hold on men's minds? Because it does fit. It may be a parable; but there is nothing there for any one to unlearn.

Secondly, I agree with Professor Nineham that to understand the Bible one needs the aid of many kinds of scholarship to know what the words meant to the writers who used them in the setting of their own times, and then considerable insight and learning to translate them into what would convey the same to us in the setting of our times. I would add, for myself, that this seems the sort of thing suitable for postgraduate study and not much before. Now if you try to teach the Bible to young children of course you tend to be driven back to 'fundamentalism' if you still insist that it has a unique authority. If you do not do that you can treat it in terms of 'stories' as we treat the stories associated with the religions of Greece and Rome. But Christians could hardly agree to that.

Let me come on now to something that will not divide Christians and secular humanists as such, but will range a minority of liberal Christian educationalists with secular humanists on the one side and the majority of less liberal Christians on the other. What is the purpose of compulsory religious education in the schools? Is it or is it not to induct children into the Christian religion? Here we come to the nub of the problem.

There are among Christians who have been thinking earnestly about this, a few, and not the least uninfluential, who advocate what they call an 'open' approach. This purpose is put very persuasively by the Rev. Allan Wainwright, Education Secretary of the British Council of Churches, in *The Times Educational Supplement* for April 16, 1965. He says:

> When we remember that most children have no significant participation in any specific Christian heritage and that home, far from countering the pressures of society, acts as a reinforcement to them, it is clear that an inducting type of religious education is quite inappropriate.
>
> On the contrary, the only justification for the inclusion of religious teaching in every school is that the issues with which it deals are of such importance that every individual ought to have the opportunity to get to grips with them: more, that all pupils should be faced with facts and ideas which force them in their turn to ask ultimate questions and seek for answers.
>
> Not to ask such questions is to be less than fully human: but in an open society such as ours, there can be no guarantee that the orthodox answers will either be reached, or, if reached, accepted.

Such a statement the secular humanist will warmly welcome. Yet there are some difficulties about it.

First, can we reconcile an 'open' approach with the Act? There is no doubt that when the Act talks of 'Worship', though it lacks the moral courage to add the necessary predicate (for you can't just worship'—you must worship someone or something), it means the worship of God as conceived by Christians. If we stick to this, we are confronted at once not with a question, but with an answer. Archbishop Beck, Roman Catholic Archbishop of Liverpool, writing in the same issue of *The Times Educational Supplement*, states the essential Christian doctrine with complete clarity. The fundamental truth is that 'God is the creator and father of all mankind' and that 'God has revealed his purpose for us in the Incarnation of his Son, Jesus Christ.' I should have thought that any Christian, whatever his denominations, would say that these were his basic beliefs too. Yet I wonder how many educated people now conceive of a 'Creator'? Rather few, I think, conceive of a Creation as a single specific act. There is some difficulty in knowing what some Protestant churchmen do believe in. Merely as a matter of reasonable use of terms (and without any argument either way) can a person who is so 'open' as to doubt whether there is a God who is a person, be described as a Christian? Is the question of the existence of a God, as Archbishop Beck, with undoubted historical warrant, uses the term, open or closed? If it is not open, very little is. The crux about the 'open' approach will be over these basic theological points. If it is agreed that the discussion be open in this sense, then it is more likely that we shall be teaching *about* religion than engaging in the teaching *of* religion. The secular humanist will of course be happy to see this change. But, logically, I think it does mean moving outside the Act, and therefore changing the Act.

Secondly, how does this suggestion of an 'open' approach accord with the facts, that is to say with present practice? What the secular humanist is concerned with is what is actually done in the schools, and what those in charge want to be done. In an earlier collection of articles about religious education in *The Times Educational Supplement* (for April 12, 1963) the first article was written by the headmistress of a secondary modern school for girls. She said:

> What is the goal of the religious instruction specialist? It is to achieve in each young person a sense of the reality of God, and some experience of worship. It is to instruct him in the faith and answer some of his intellectual doubts and difficulties.

There is no hesitancy about that. It is indoctrination pure and simple. It begs every question that should be open. It does not seek answers, it claims to know them in advance. It does not consider doubts with intellectual candour, it provides an armoury from which they can be disposed of. As that admirable columnist Peter Quince said in the *Teacher* (December 7, 1962), in an age of appeals to mass credulity by advertisers and propagandists of all kinds, teachers are bound to encourage children

> to seek out the motives behind unsupported statements and to question the authority on which they are made. . . . They feel they must warn children that there never has been a time when it was so important not to take statements on trust but to examine everything critically in the light of logic and tried experience. But the schools cannot speak with two voices. They cannot teach children how to look at life critically in lessons on civics and current affairs, and urge them to be uncritical in religious instruction.

What complicates things is that some of the Christian educationalists who favour the 'open' approach are attached to traditional language and images. (The secular humanist is of course in the easier position here. If you take the Bible as literature, and not as 'truth' in the propositional sense, you can prefer the language of the King James Bible to any modern version that might recommend itself to a modern theological conscience rather better.) No one would want to be self-righteously purist about the reconciliation of attitudes that seem right to us now with traditional forms, in any walk of life. Some accommodation is not only to be expected, but is to be valued where the tradition has beauty or historic appeal. Yet one must draw the line somewhere. I was brought up to honour the Old Testament Jews who would not bow the knee to Baal, and the early Christians who suffered martyrdom rather than offer incense to the image of the Emperor. Were they wrong? Was it very unsophisticated not to understand that the image of the Emperor expressed a most valuable tradition, that of peace and order within the Empire? There were Fellows of

Colleges in the nineteenth century who felt they must resign their fellowships for doubts that some modern churchmen seem able to take gaily in their stride. They seem able to recite the creeds and say out loud in public that they believe Jesus was delivered from the virgin's womb and tell us afterwards that of course they don't believe in the virgin birth. And these are the people whose honesty of mind one would not think in the ordinary way of impugning and who seem to have come to an honest accommodation with themselves. I confess to some difficulty in trying, on the one hand, not to be censorious, and on the other feeling the traditional nonconformist rising up with great force within me. What did Swift, after he had become a Dean, make of his Tale of a Tub?

However this may be, there is no doubt that when you make what seems to be a factual proposition to children they understand it in that way. They will not have the skill to follow the subtleties of these reconciliations. If you do not want to give the impression that you are making propositional statements, if you wish to be understood to be in the world of 'as if', you can rely with much confidence on the capacity of children to discriminate, even though the 'temporary suspension of disbelief' may be subtly different from what it would be in a mature mind. Children 'believe' in fairy stories as adults don't. They suspend disbelief with greater imaginative intensity, and no doubt their distinction between fact and fantasy is not what it will later become. But they understand when you are telling them a fairy story or a myth. The most they do is sometimes to ask to make sure. If you are telling them the myths of Greece they may perhaps ask if Apollo really existed (though I think they rarely need to), but I know of no child who has been converted to Greek religion because we tell them so many of its stories. But when stories are told from the Bible, teachers do not use the same tone of voice, do not give the same impression, that they would if they were telling stories associated with other religions or with myths of a pagan kind. To the secular humanist, however interesting or valuable these stories may be as vehicles of human experience, they are essentially of the same kind as all the other great systems of myths by which earlier man tried to express his awareness of the universe and of mankind. Now we are so clear about the non-authoritative standing of, say, Homer in matters of propositional statement that we have no difficulty. The finer his language the finer our experience. But it was not so for Plato, for the battle about Homer's authority was not then won. For us the analogue is the traditional language of the Christian religion. For those who are 'open' about the authority of the Bible in propositional matters—as for Plato and Homer—the more powerful the language the greater the possibility of error. If, as we have seen, a proper understanding of the Bible is a difficult and scholarly matter and the teachers are driven back to fundamentalism, the educational danger cannot be ignored. The example of the position of evolutionary biology is the most obvious one. It is still by no means assured in parts of the United States where fundamentalists, Protestant or Catholic, can influence teaching and texts.

We are familiar with the stock answer to this sort of criticism : that there is not really an antithesis between the procedures in religious education and those for other studies. The modes are not antithetic, only different. This argument needs careful examination. We know historically that a great deal that is no longer believed by an educated person (witchcraft, for example) for long had religious sanction. Poor Sir Thomas Browne got into a sad confusion over this same mattter of witchcraft and one wonders if this was the reason that, for all his scientific curiosity, he was never invited to become a member of the Royal Society. He was confused because he believed that there were two kinds of Truth, truth and Higher Truth. This theme has been taken up very much in our own time, and the (to me) quite decisive destructive account of it is to be found in Miss Kathleen Nott's book, 'The Emperor's Clothes'. In fact, more and more people as education has spread, have acted in their daily lives as humanists, adopting for all practical daily purposes the cause-and-effect assumptions. They have of course continued to understand the difference between the modes of discourse of science and poetry, but what is there in a supposed religious mode of discourse that is not either 'scientific' (improperly) or 'poetic' (properly, if the imaginative pressure and the expression are fine enough)? At all events we can clearly say that the propositional statements of religion, in so far as they affect our daily lives, are increasingly less regarded. Whole areas of religious 'experience' have thus dropped out. One might ask, without raising the question of the existence of God, what has happened to the Devil, and why? As a supposed person—and he has been very much that to the overwhelming majority of Christians in history—he has just disappeared, leaving of course something of a logical vacuum. And in what we ordinarily call matters of fact, historical or scientific, few Christians accord the Bible any special authority (which, of course, is not to say that nothing stated in it happened; we come to a conclusion about that, however, on historical or scientific grounds, not those of revelation). But the position has not quite been achieved, and religious teaching in the schools tends to be regressive, not progressive in this.

In the same recent number of *The Times Educational Supplement* from which I have quoted, Mr Norman Bull, of St Luke's College, Exeter writes:

> The incessant 'is it true' of the older junior is the opportunity to show how truth, far too immense a concept to be limited to mere historicity—though there are those who propagate such a heresy—is mediated in different forms, each conveying truth in its own right.

Now, if I may say so, I think he is in some danger here. What is 'mere' historicity? Does he mean that we can assert that something is historically true when as sober historians we should very seriously doubt it? That we are not to apply fully historical criteria to what claim to be historical statements? And how does one distinguish between religious statements that have the form of historical statements but that really belong to another mode of truth which exists in its own right? When Gibbon, in a very famous chapter, pointed out that although there were many very competent chroniclers and observers at the time, none seems to have noticed that darkness covered the earth for some hours at the crucifixion of Jesus, was he indulging in mere historicity? If a child asked Mr Bull if it was true that darkness did cover the earth at this time, the sense in which he was using the word 'true' would be perfectly plain, and there would be only one honest answer: No, so far as we can tell, it did not. I think Mr Bull would feel he had to give that answer. This is where the area of difficulty lies, and one detects a perpetual reluctance to make the clean break which to the secular humanist seems right and bound to be made by any one who is seeing clearly. If the question were, say, whether Job actually existed one could say that this did not matter at all. If there were no such actual person the value of that remarkable book would be no more affected than the value of Hamlet would be if we decided that there never had been such a person in history. But will the teachers of religious education in school say frankly that Adam and Eve have in this respect the same status as Hamlet, that the sun never did stand still for Joshua to win a battle, that you can't turn water into wine by a magical command, that some people think that the idea of a Christian personal God has more in common with other ideas of God in which no one now believes than it has with statements of fact? The learned and liberal may be impatient with me for dwelling on these things, but I said that by religious education for the purpose of this paper, I meant what goes on under that name in schools, and I think I am nearer to that in what I am criticizing than their scholarly theology is.

The key question is of course, as Peter Quince pointed out, whether or not the critical faculty that is nourished in all good teaching in other school subjects is to be inhibited in religious education by what is quite clearly in practice, though no doubt in different degrees in different places, a resort to answers given on authority. The secular humanist has a considerable confidence that things are moving his way. As I have said, for almost all areas of practical life now we do adopt criteria derived from human experience. That is one reason why, whatever we call ourselves, we can work in practice so well together—and as on the whole we do. A community development worker in a very pre-technical society has to be conscious of supernaturalist beliefs and taboos that may affect anything he does. With us, we don't even bother to ascertain the religious beliefs of our doctor, or of our farm-workers, or of anybody else. Even in education, though differences may indeed be evident in outlook and practice, we can discuss together how a child develops and what that implies, whether we have any religion or not. Only a hundred years ago we were much less humanist in practice and daily conduct in the classroom was much more governed by views of human nature derived from religious dogma. So long, therefore, as this process of distancing the supernatural is allowed to continue without repressive interference, the secular humanist will not be unduly worried. He probably will not agitate over much—though perhaps he ought —to get the religious education period removed, though I think he will agitate to have something done about the 'act of worship' in the mornings. The one thing that should not be tolerated is intolerance. But for the rest, let discussion continue.

But there is one area where we cannot just say that. It is an area in which I am sure we must think and act with much greater speed and vigour than we are showing yet. This is the area of moral education. I know I speak for a good number of secular humanists when I say that we are very anxious to get Christians to agree with us (without abandoning their religious position for themselves) that in a society where religious authority does not run for the population as a whole moral education must be put on the basis of what has been found to be good in human life; and that moral education (whatever name might be given to it) should be recognized as existing in its own right and not as virtually identical with religious education.

There is really urgent need for action about the role of the school in moral education. Let me of course make clear that I am not one of those who go round lamenting the terrible state of modern youth and sigh for the return of the days of Queen Victoria. I suspect such people of being unhistorical. I feel sure that if they could be taken back to the slums and alleys of the industrial cities of the last century they would return to us, even with our 'mods' and 'rockers', with an immense sigh of relief. If they presume to speak for modern youth as a whole I am sure they are libelling them. But there is a problem, and not least for the schools.

The nature of this problem is seen clearly by Mr Wainwright, whom I have already quoted. He says:

> Too close an association between religious education and moral education may, paradoxically, be harmful rather than beneficial. Granted that the best basis for morals is religious, if religion is rejected, then a secular basis for morals becomes essential.

In a sense to ask Christians to take this position, not for their private philosophy, but for practical advocacy, would seem to be asking very little. If a Christian believes certain things to be good he may put it to himself that this is in accordance with a divine will; but it would be surprising if he did not believe that it could also be shown to be good in terms of considered human experience. When he is talking with young people for whom a religious sanction does not hold we are saying simply that he should rest his case on these grounds, which should be sufficient, whatever he might personally add. Would not this be in the tradition that when speaking with those outside a faith one speaks in terms of the natural law? Unless this is done, what is happening will continue to happen: the majority of listeners will not be impressed and moral education will in large measure go by default.

Why should there be any difficulty about this? The religious missionary has formed a certain habit of mind which drives him back to the appeal to authority when human experience is not easy to sum up or to discuss patiently. Ethical situations, especially those between particular persons in particular circumstances, rarely fit neatly into some resounding authoritative generalization. As we can see all too well from the pronouncements of moralizing judges about unhappy persons who come before them, the Law (whether that of a state or a church) is a very blunt instrument. This is increasingly realized by the young. For very many of them, for instance, the choice is not to be stated in terms of categorical opposites, like no intercourse at all before marriage and intercourse virtually without discrimination. An authoritarian ban will not impress them. But who is to blame if we do not make clear that moral obliquity is not to be so crudely decided on authority. We can say to follow this example that some would still think complete abstinence right, but to suggest that the only alternative that can be taken by a person trying to be responsible is promiscuity is to make them feel that we are insulting their intelligence. Let all views be put, but in terms of what is humanly good. For this is the only basis many of them will accept. What we have to do is to form in every young man and woman, so far as we can, an ethical sensitiveness and a critical discrimination that will enable them to form a sound judgement in action, in action in circumstances that may well differ too much to come under a sweeping generalization. The boy or girl who grows up with moral standards in this sense will in reality be a more moral person, because he understands the need for discrimination between good and evil, than one who automatically obeys a general injunction. In any case, they will not now obey it. How can the young be encouraged to feel for the moral realities in every situation?

If you cannot do this by blind adherence to a law, no more can you do it unless you do form for yourself practical norms. Now it is here that those who lament have some reason on their side. Moral conduct may have been worse in the general population a hundred years ago, but there was less question as to what were the proper standards. It is true that we are throwing too much responsibility on the young now in expecting them to discover themselves morally without the norms that we could give them more securely. The question is: where do we find those norms if we ourselves question formerly accepted standards so much?

As I have argued elsewhere, this is less difficult than our disagreement over certain questions of conduct might lead us to suppose, and much less difficult than we might suppose from our disagreement in matters of religion. There is in our society a very considerable consensus as to what is good behaviour and what is not, and as to what constitutes a good man or woman. Where we disagree is much less about our values in practice than about explanations of where our values come from. I can think of nothing more practical than bringing up the young to be moral adult men and women, and if in fact we largely agree about what being a good person is, why cannot we unite to do what is so obviously needed in the schools?

The first difficulty—a clearing-the-ground difficulty—is to get people to understand what Mr Wainwright has said, and to act upon it. I cannot commit him, but I would say for myself that this means, even though we make no change in the stipulation for a religious education period in the school, the establishment of moral education, on a human basis, in its own right. This means, of course, much more than desultory discussions about problems in a free period. It means something thought out, and to the extent necessary structured, in a programme of discussion and study. The period of religious education could be transformed into this, as the Crowther Report half-suggested. But this is not really satisfactory. Religious education and moral education are not identical and interchangeable, and I take it that when the Act said religious instruction it meant religious instruction. But apart from that, what I am advocating is not apparently 'open' moral education

under the specialist in religious education and really under the auspices still of religion. I mean something in its own right, taught by teachers of the right experience and with the right approach, whatever their personal attitude to religion. So important do many humanists feel this establishment of moral education to be that if Christian believers would combine forces with them to do what is needed on the only basis that will work they would, without hiding their other views, be very ready to put more of their energies into this than in getting the religious education period as such abolished.

Let me attempt to sum up what I have been saying. I have argued that the question of religious education in the schools is not in the first place an argument about religion, but an argument about fairness between people with different beliefs in our very mixed society, and that the privileged position, amounting almost to a monopoly, accorded at present to an 'orthodox' minority cannot be defended in democratic principle and leads to a good deal of unfair pressure, and of hypocrisy in practice. Secondly, I have welcomed those Christian educationalists who say they would like an 'open' approach in religious education and believe that this would be very much better than what we have at present, though I do see some difficulties about it. I have suggested that there is a good deal of difference between what liberal-minded Christians and scholars think and talk about and what actually is done in the schools. What normally takes place, I have suggested, is indoctrination, often at a pretty low intellectual level. And, lastly, I have said that although we could perhaps feel that these things will be resolved through discussion in the course of time, there is one thing that we cannot continue to mishandle, and that is the moral education of our young people. I have argued that precisely because we live in a society in which only a minority are going to respond to a religious sanction for moral behaviour we must place our discussions as to conduct on the basis of what human experience shows to be good and not good, and I have suggested that if we would only make up our minds to combine for these practical purposes, whatever our differences of ultimate philosophy, we could do so much more easily and happily than our divisions about religion would lead us to suppose. And I have urged that in the interests of our young people we need *very much* to do this.

CHAPTER XI

CONCLUSIONS AND RECOMMENDATIONS

ALEXANDER WEDDERSPOON

Part One: Conference Recommendations

It should be made clear that this was a study conference conducted under the auspices of a university department of education. Membership was by invitation only and was inevitably limited. Every effort was made to ensure that the membership should be as representative as possible. Invitations were extended to teachers all over the British Isles and at every level of the educational system from university to primary school. To our loss, and for reasons which were personal not professional, none of the primary school head or assistant teachers invited to the conference accepted the invitation. Careful enquiry revealed that over one quarter of the members of the conference had experience of teaching in primary schools and were in regular contact with them. Only one of the twenty recommendations, however, specifically relates to religious education in the primary school. This element of under-representation, though regrettable and unavoidable, can therefore scarcely be regarded as a serious invalidation of the findings of the conference.

Financial and administrative considerations limited the membership to approximately 100. It should be appreciated that there were very many other men and women working in the field of religious education to whom the organizers of the conference would have wished to extend invitations had circumstances enabled them to do so.

The membership consisted of:

21 lecturers in university departments of Education in England and Wales, and colleges of education in Scotland.
24 principals and lecturers in teacher training colleges.
30 head teachers and assistant teachers in secondary schools of all kinds, Grammar Comprehensive, Secondary Modern, and Public Independent.
10 representatives of the education committees of the churches
10 HM inspectors and LEA inspectors.
6 Members of Parliament, research students, and others.

There was also a small but highly articulate delegation of four from the British Humanist Association. They contributed astringently and intelligently to the discussions, but would naturally not wish to be formally associated with the recommendations.

All but six members of the conference were practising educators whose work or special interests lay in the field of religious education. Members were divided into five discussion groups. Written records were made of their discussions by secretaries working from shorthand notes or tape recordings. Six hours were devoted to group discussion. These recommendations, therefore, represent the outcome of thirty hours of discussion.

Members were deliberately not given advance notice of the subjects to be discussed. It was hoped that by confronting them with some of the basic questions facing religious education they would speak what was uppermost in their minds—what they really felt in the light of their day to day experience. The questions set for discussion were not abstruse points in theology or educational theory such as would require careful previous thought and study. They were some of the basic questions which any thoughtful and responsible person professionally engaged in religious education must perpetually face, e.g. the aims of religious education; content of the Agreed

Syllabus; staffing problems, etc. These recommendations must be accepted for what they are—the opinions, feelings and ideas of 100 practising educators on some of the more fundamental problems of religious education twenty years after the 1944 Education Act became effective. The members of the conference would not wish the significance of their views to be over-estimated. On the other hand, the responsibly expressed opinions of 100 professionals must represent a contribution which all giving thought for the future of religious education in England and Wales would hardly wish to neglect.

Part One of this chapter consists of the recommendations made by the conference. These represent the outcome of the discussions and findings of the groups, edited with the greatest possible objectivity. Nothing *has* been included which cannot be supported by reference to the shorthand notes. Quotations have been made from these notes exactly as they stand— some in direct speech, some in reported speech, and some ungrammatical.

Part Two of this chapter, 'On to 1984' consists of an editorial commentary on the recommendations. Only in this part of the chapter has the editor felt in any way free to express his own personal views. This point must be clearly understood. In writing the conclusions of any conference, there is a danger that the editor may insinuate his own personal opinions by the way in which he presents and comments upon the material. Others may then find statements and opinions attributed to them which they did not express. The division of this chapter into two separate parts is intended to prevent this possibility.

Section A. Principal Recommendations

The following recommendations are drawn from the discussions and findings of *all five* groups. Where group findings are in disagreement, this is stated.

1. THE AIMS OF RELIGIOUS EDUCATION IN THE COUNTY SCHOOL UNDER THE 1944 ACT ARE FUNDAMENTALLY EDUCATIONAL.

The following quotations illustrate what members understood by this.

'Religious education is not indoctrination, it is an attempt to meet the spiritual needs of children.'

'The aim is surely to give children a core of knowledge and experience so that they don't leave school ignorant of what Christianity stands for, but it is not the teacher's business to proselytize, but to present Christianity attractively so they can choose.'

'. . . surely there is also a negative aim—removing false concepts of what Christianity stands for picked up from popular media.'

'It is the discussion of the problems of man's profoundest concern.'

'We are trying to give them a chance to make up their minds for themselves, but not leaving their minds so wide open that they have nothing to make up.'

Members also commented on the influence of religious education in moral education:

'. . . is not our aim to present to children the possibility of a religious interpretation of life which is going to affect various sides of their character and personality?'

'The boy should be enabled to know God, and to know himself in relation to God and to view moral issues from this standpoint.'

Many members appeared emphatic that the aims of religious education in the county schools were not ecclesiastical:

'It was felt that it was an abuse of the Act to seek to make converts, but that it was possible to state the Christian interpretation of life, and its link with the eternal without doing this.'

'It's not the school's job to make church members.'

2. A CLEAR MAJORITY FELT THAT RELIGIOUS INSTRUCTION SHOULD CONTINUE TO BE GIVEN IN SCHOOLS UNDER THE EXISTING STATUTORY ARRANGEMENTS.

All the groups agreed that religious instruction should continue to be given in schools.

Three of the five agreed that it should continue under existing statutory arrangements.

Two of the groups felt that some modification of the 'compulsory' requirement might be desirable. One of these two groups, however, qualified their recommendations by suggesting that the 'compulsory' requirement could be removed when the subject had become so well staffed and so well established as to render any 'compulsory' requirement superfluous.

3. RESEARCH FINDINGS SINCE 1944 HAVE REPEATEDLY STRESSED THE SHORTAGE OF QUALIFIED RELIGIOUS EDUCATION TEACHERS. AN ACUTE STAFFING CRISIS NOW EXISTS. A JOINT EXECUTIVE BODY REQUIRES TO BE SET UP WITHOUT DELAY TO EXAMINE AND ACT UPON THIS AS A MATTER OF URGENCY. THIS BODY SHOULD BE REPRESENTATIVE OF THE SCHOOLS, THE CHURCHES, THE DEPARTMENT OF EDUCATION AND SCIENCE, AND THE TEACHER TRAINING INSTITUTIONS. IT MUST BE REPRESENTATIVE ENOUGH TO ENSURE RESPECT AND SMALL ENOUGH TO ENSURE ACTION. IT IS IDLE TO SUPPOSE THAT RELIGIOUS EDUCATION CAN EFFECTIVELY CONTINUE AS A LIVE OPTION IN THE SCHOOLS UNLESS THIS STAFFING CRISIS IS RESOLVED. THE CONFERENCE AGREED THAT THIS WAS THE ONE MOST OBVIOUS PRACTICAL NEED FOR RELIGIOUS EDUCATION IN BRITAIN IN THE FORESEEABLE FUTURE.

The following quotations are sufficient to illustrate this recommendation, on which there was very widespread agreement.

'The urgent need to get more people who are trained as religious education specialists is paramount.'

'The group was in complete agreement that a joint consultative body should be set up.'

'To gain support for its measures . . . the joint consultative body will have to concern itself with teachers for all children, not just teachers for grammar schools.'

N

'I have to try and teach 800 children in a week. Whatever my aims and methods, it will look in the end as if nothing has been achieved.'

4. THE OVERWHELMING MAJORITY OF MEMBERS OF THE CONFERENCE WERE AGREED THAT FACILITIES FOR SCHOOL WORSHIP SHOULD CONTINUE TO BE PROVIDED. THREE OF THE GROUPS RECOMMENDED THAT SOME MODIFICATION OF THE 'COMPULSORY' REQUIREMENT REGARDING WORSHIP MIGHT BE DESIRABLE. TWO OF THE GROUPS RECOMMENDED THAT THE EXISTING STATUTORY ARRANGEMENTS SHOULD BE RETAINED.

A large number of practical suggestions were discussed. Very widespread and outspoken dissatisfaction was expressed at the quality of much school worship. The following selection of comments will illustrate the variety of views expressed. Many members suggested changes in the organization and conduct of school assembly.

'Do we not think that a distinction should be made between daily assembly and daily worship?'

'Instead of being first thing every morning should not assembly take place say once a week in church?'

'School assembly could take place without worship, and then have worship properly on its own, separate from administration and discipline.'

Some were very dubious about letting older children decide for themselves whether or not to attend assembly:

'When I discussed this question with my girls, they preferred that assembly should be kept compulsory, for if it was made optional they wouldn't go.'

'It was felt that allowing children to opt out would not be entirely satisfactory. Many children would not come because their friends did not come.'

'Are we not touching on a more basic question here—the whole question of authority in education. If children are allowed to choose this and choose that, where does the process end? And how is the ethos of the school to be preserved?'

Other members criticized the way in which many assemblies were conducted and the surroundings in which they took place, feeling that this is what lies at the root of the whole issue:

'Nothing is to be gained by change. The whole trouble is that good assemblies are good and bad are bad. This is the real difficulty.'

'Children are sometimes inoculated against worship by the attitude of the people who are taking assembly.'

5. AGREED SYLLABUSES OF RELIGIOUS INSTRUCTION ARE NECESSARY AND SHOULD BE RETAINED. THE MAJORITY OF AGREED SYLLABUSES IN USE REQUIRE REVISION IN FORM AND CONTENT. THE STANDING ADVISORY COUNCIL ON RELIGIOUS EDUCATION IN EACH LOCAL AUTHORITY SHOULD EXAMINE THE SYLLABUS CURRENTLY IN USE BY THAT AUTHORITY. IF NO ACTION HAS BEEN TAKEN IN THE RECENT PAST, IMMEDIATE STEPS SHOULD BE TAKEN TO REVISE THE SYLLABUS IN THE LIGHT OF CONTEMPORARY SCHOLARSHIP AND EDUCATIONAL PRACTICE. ACTION SHOULD ALSO BE TAKEN TO ENSURE THAT THE SYLLABUS IS KEPT UNDER REGULAR REVIEW.

Many members criticized the inactivity and unconcern shown in this matter by some Local Authorities. This whole theme provoked extensive discussion. The following extracts illustrate some of the main points. The need for revision:

'The syllabuses need radical modification, but let us retain them.'

'It really is important that an Agreed Syllabus is kept under regular review, or it very easily becomes sterotyped.'

'It emerged from recent research on the London syllabus that most teachers felt that there was a need for radical reform. Non-specialists in particular had asked for more guidance.'

These comments illustrate some of the ways in which members would wish to see the syllabuses revised:

'Agreed Syllabuses have been far too dominated by the activities of the grammar school; packed with subject matter for informed Christians rather than what was relevant and capable of being understood. We could give a general answer here that the interests of the children have been under-regarded in the framing of agreed syllabuses. The adult concerned with subject matter has been far too much in the centre of the picture.'

'I think we spend far too much time on the Old Testament with these children. It confuses them. It is clear from our experience that we should spend more time on the New Testament.'

'No one Agreed Syllabus is adequate for the varied needs of so many different types of secondary schools.'

'The group felt that there was a need for a shift of emphasis from content to approach and presentation. The question of the relevance of the Bible to life today should be seen to be central.'

'The starting point must still be the Christian religion, but other religions can no longer be ignored.'

'A great deal of what has been suggested for religious instruction in schools has really been a course for theological students.'

'What's the point of children knowing about the baby in the bulrushes if they've no idea what is meant by the Christian life?'

'A more open-ended approach may be all right, so long as it does not result in empty-mindedness.'

Members appeared to have little confidence in the effectiveness of the existing administrative machinery for the revision of Agreed Syllabuses. One grammar school headmaster is recorded as describing the Standing Advisory Council on Religious Education in his Local Education Authority as:

'. . . hopeless. Just a dead duck.'

6. TEACHERS OF RELIGIOUS EDUCATION IN THE PRIMARY SCHOOL REQUIRE MORE ADEQUATE AND RELEVANT THEOLOGICAL PREPARATION. A MOVEMENT TOWARDS SOME ELEMENT OF SPECIALIZATION IN THE PRIMARY SCHOOLS WAS RECOGNIZED.

Members commented on the difficult and often profound

nature of the questions which primary school children frequently asked:

'The class was found on a Monday morning all drawing pictures of coffins. Questioning revealed that the children had all been watching the funeral of Sir Winston Churchill on television. "Where is he now, miss?" they asked.'

'A nine year old boy in a junior school asked if Christ would still have been born if the birth pill had been available in the first century and if the Virgin Mary had taken it.'

Answering questions such as these requires adequate training both in theology and psychology:

'You need just as much theology for teaching in the junior school as anywhere else.'

'There is a tremendous need on the part of primary teachers for a deeper understanding of both theological problems and child psychology.'

'It is the class teacher who teaches religious education in the primary school, and lectures in college are not well attended. Small wonder they often fall back on fundamentalism.'

Many members commented on the contribution which the specialist could make in the primary school:

'Attention was drawn to the fact that there were very few specialist teachers of religious education in the primary school, and this intensified the problem. There were two difficulties; selection of the correct stories, and the correct approach to the stories.'

'The curriculum in the primary school is almost entirely biblical, but the Bible ought not to be taught indiscriminately.'

'The fact is that what looks like difficult material in the Bible is quite suitable for young children if it is interpreted properly.'

'There is a danger in the primary school of teaching too much too soon and Bible stories have to be carefully selected to link up with the children's interests and experience.'

'Concepts which are too adult are being taught by methods which are too babyish.'

7. THE RESEARCH INTO RELIGIOUS THINKING IN CHILDHOOD CONDUCTED BY DR R. W. GOLDMAN WAS WELCOMED AS A USEFUL INITIAL CONTRIBUTION. VERY MUCH MORE RESEARCH OF THIS KIND IS REQUIRED. IF FULLY SUBSTANTIATED IT COULD LEAD TO CHANGES IN THE PRACTICE OF RELIGIOUS EDUCATION, NOT LEAST IN THE PRIMARY SCHOOL.

This appears to have been widely discussed, but the hesitancy felt by many members is apparent in the following extracts:

'Some members commented on the incompleteness of Dr Goldman's researches, but others pointed out that his studies in this field have only just begun.'

'Another member felt that he must suspend his judgment until Dr Goldman's next book appears.'

'I find it incredible that there have been children since the start of time, yet it appears we only understand them now that Dr Goldman has come along.'

8. IMMEDIATE EXAMINATION IS REQUIRED OF WHAT CONSTI-TUTES A 'THEOLOGICAL QUALIFICATION' FOR THOSE WHO INTEND TO BECOME TEACHERS. THE CONTENTS OF MANY UNIVER-SITY AND TRAINING COLLEGE COURSES IN THEOLOGY WERE CRITICIZED AS EXCESSIVELY HISTORICAL AND LINGUISTIC AND UNRELATED TO CONTEMPORARY INTELLECTUAL CONCERNS.

Irrelevance was the charge most commonly laid against the university courses in theology:

'We really need to reorientate our whole ideas about theology —there is far too much Hebrew and textual criticism and far too little theolgical thought which is really relevant.'

'The University theology faculties will have to see their way to a much wider and more relevant approach.'

'Successful teaching in the fifth and sixth forms depends on the teacher having a grasp of the philosophy of religion and Christian ethics—all too often this is what he never learnt.'

'University courses in theology were heavily attacked by all members of the group.'

Training college courses in divinity came in for similar comments:

'Some of our students lack confidence even before a class of nine year olds because they simply do not know their stuff. Standards require a good deal of stiffening, especially in the Divinity Main courses.'

'I am just not happy about much of the work done in training colleges, especially in those colleges where there is a division between 'education' and the teaching of the academic subjects. This dichotomy is thoroughly bad, especially for divinity teaching.'

On the whole question, one of the humanists commented:
'All our best atheists got prizes for Scripture.'

9. A SERIOUS FAILURE OF COMMUNICATION EXISTS BETWEEN THE WORK OF THEOLOGIANS IN UNIVERSITIES AND THE WORK OF RELIGIOUS EDUCATION TEACHERS IN SCHOOLS. THE UNIVERSITY INSTITUTES OF EDUCATION, EXTRA-MURAL DEPARTMENTS, LOCAL EDUCATION AUTHORITIES, AND THE CHRISTIAN EDUCATION MOVEMENT, ARE URGED TO PROVIDE REGULAR COURSES TO PRESERVE CONTACT BETWEEN THESE TWO GROUPS OF TEACHERS WHOSE WORK IS IN MANY WAYS INTER-RELATED.

The following extracts will be adequate to illustrate this widely expressed recommendation:

'It is true that a serious gap exists between the academic theologians and the teachers, but isn't this equally true in other faculties?'

'The group expressed concern at the inaccessibility of academic theologians and sought greater liaison.'

'The trouble seems to me to be that too few people are doing any real theology. The academics withdraw into their researches and the teachers into fundamentalism.'

'It was pointed out that what made *Honest to God* the success it was with the general public was that it made theology relevant to people who would not normally discuss it.'

'There is a need for more intermediaries and middle-men.'

10. SOME PLACE COULD BE GIVEN IN RELIGIOUS EDUCATION DISCUSSIONS IN THE SIXTH FORM TO INTELLIGENT AND RE-SPONSIBLE DISCUSSION OF THE STANDPOINT OF SECULAR AGNOSTICISM.

This subject provoked shorter discussion than was anticipated. Few of the teachers present felt it their business to make any attempt positively to introduce the subject in sixth form discussion :

'The group doubted whether it would be the responsibility of a Christian to introduce this standpoint in a religious education period when he himself did not agree with it.'

Most members felt that secular agnosticism should be fully and frankly discussed when it arose :

'The question should not be consciously introduced, but should be dealt with when the children ask questions, as with any other thing.'

'Isn't there some danger in using labels like this? Surely all good religious education teaching will provoke agnostic questions?'

A distinction was recognized between thinking and unthinking agnosticism :

'My lot don't need to be introduced to secular agnosticism, they are agnostics already.'

But one of the humanists present observed :

'The unthinking agnosticism and rejection of religion that the modern world exhibits clearly impinges on all children, but is not the same as positive well thought out descriptions of non-Christian positions and attitudes.'

The idea of the 'open society' gained little support and criticism was expressed of the whole humanist standpoint :

'It was agreed that an 'open society' meant in general the right of parents to give their children their own world view.'

'Do we live in such an "open society"? I think this is one of many humanist false assumptions.'

11. CLOSER RELATIONSHIPS SHOULD BE DEVELOPED BETWEEN THE SCHOOLS AND THE CHURCHES. THIS MAY BEST BE DONE ECUMENICALLY AT A LOCAL LEVEL THROUGH COUNCILS OF CHURCHES.

This recommendation was made by four out of the five groups, and was discussed by the fifth. A wide variety of practical suggestions were also discussed.

Many members severely criticized the Churches for their apparent lack of interest and concern for the work of religious education in the county schools:

'The Churches are doing nothing like enough in this whole field.'

'They have got to show much more concern for the seriousness of the situation.'

'The Churches are not helping by holding teaching as an important vocation. They could help here, putting it over to young people, but they are not interested.'

'Some clergy seem to take the trouble of getting in touch with their local schools and making contacts, but others seem neither to know nor care.'

Members emphasized how very many children were completely out of contact with the Churches and knew nothing about them.

It was widely felt that this was a problem to be tackled ecumenically, at a local level:

'There should be an education sub-committee of the local council of churches to which both parents and teachers could refer.'

'There is a great need to establish working links between schools and churches. Very little positive action is being taken about this.'

'Perhaps the Churches could provide technical knowledge

and help for the schools when requested—clergy acting in an advisory capacity.'

'School leavers should be interviewed by the local clergy on leaving—they could talk to children of their denomination, and encourage them to join youth clubs, etc.'

Nor did the theological issue pass unnoticed:

'Teachers of religious education must expect to be more and more alone in the future; surely the issue is a theological one, and what we want the Church to be saying to the teachers is, "You are the Church".'

12. THE QUALITY OF TEACHING IN MANY CHURCH SUNDAY SCHOOLS REQUIRES IMMEDIATE IMPROVEMENT.

This view was widely expressed. Many members commented on the confusing effect which poor quality Sunday school teaching could have on religious education in the county schools. The following two extracts are very typical:

'There is a great need for consultation between church bodies and the schools, particularly in relation to the Sunday schools. Untrained and amateur Sunday school teachers are a problem, and difference between what was taught at school and at Sunday school creates difficulties for the children.'

'There is too much shoddy Sunday school teaching, because the Churches are relying on the schools to do something which only the Church can do.'

13. THE NEED EXISTS FOR A NATIONAL ASSOCIATION OF RE-LIGIOUS EDUCATION TEACHERS.

This recommendation was very widely expressed, and the following extract is typical of many others:

'The business of teaching religious education is the business of the teacher and there ought to be an association for religious education teachers similar to the Science Masters Association, which does superb work.'

Section B

The following subsidiary recommendations were made by

individual groups. In using the classification 'subsidiary', no comment is implied on the value of the recommendations. The distinction is only made because they do not appear to have been discussed by all five groups.

1. LOCAL EDUCATION AUTHORITIES ARE URGED TO APPOINT FULL TIME ADVISERS ON RELIGIOUS EDUCATION.

Strongly recommended by three groups.

2. SCHOOLS REQUIRE TO MAKE A POINT OF DRAWING THE ATTENTION OF PARENTS TO THEIR RIGHTS TO WITHDRAW THEIR CHILDREN UNDER THE CONSCIENCE CLAUSES OF THE 1944 ACT.

Recommended by two groups.

3. RELIGIOUS AND EDUCATIONAL PUBLISHERS ARE STRONGLY URGED TO GIVE MORE ATTENTION TO THE PROVISION OF LITERATURE AND TEXT BOOKS SUITABLE FOR RELIGIOUS EDUCATION IN SCHOOLS. THE NEED IS PARTICULARLY APPARENT IN SECONDARY SCHOOLS.

Recommended by two groups.

4. SOME ENQUIRY IS NECESSARY INTO THE EFFECTIVENESS OF THE PRESENT METHODS OF TRAINING RELIGIOUS EDUCATION TEACHERS. CRITICISM WAS PARTICULARLY EXPRESSED OF THE NATURE AND CONTENT OF TRAINING COURSES IN THE UNIVERSITY DEPARTMENTS OF EDUCATION.

Recommended by two groups.

5. GCE 'O' AND 'A' LEVEL SYLLABUSES IN RELIGIOUS KNOWLEDGE REQUIRE REVISION IN FORM AND CONTENT.

Recommended by one group.

6. CLERGY AND MINISTERS EMPLOYED AS RELIGIOUS EDUCATION TEACHERS IN SCHOOLS REQUIRE TRAINING AS TEACHERS. THIS TRAINING MAY BE EITHER FULL TIME, SHORT COURSE, OR IN-SERVICE, BUT IS ESSENTIAL.

Recommended by one group.

7. ORDINANDS IN THE CHURCH OF ENGLAND AND THE FREE CHURCHES REQUIRE MORE SERIOUS PREPARATION IN THE PRINCIPLES AND METHODS OF RELIGIOUS EDUCATION.

Recommended by one group.

Part Two: On to 1984

The significance of the recommendations made in Part One of this Chapter will be self evident to all who are professionally engaged in religious education. This report will, however, be read by many parents and others to whom they may not be so clear. This part of the Chapter provides some of the necessary explanatory material. It also includes such comment of my own as I believe to be relevant. I have not attempted to express the 'mind of the conference' on any issue, and no one should be held responsible for the views expressed in this part of the Chapter other than myself.

I should like to stress again a point made in the introduction—that this report is mainly concerned with the practice of religious education; the conditions which make for educational effectiveness. It is not concerned with the equally important need for re-statement of principle. This was attempted in the 1965 Hibbert Lectures, *Christianity in Education*, to which reference has already been made. This report should not, therefore, be criticized for failing to achieve what it does not set out to attempt.

The Aims of Religious Education

'In these days when men are apt to associate education predominantly with the state, it is useful to remind ourselves that our English schools were the creation of the Church and took their rise almost at the same time as the introduction of Christianity into this island.'[1] Before 1870, the aims of religious education in English schools were frankly ecclesiastical, as might be expected when the vast majority of schools were maintained by the Churches. 'The National Society' is the tactful abbreviation now in use for the name of one of the voluntary bodies most active in the establishment of elementary schools in the nineteenth century. But the full title then given to the society was, 'The National Society for Promoting the Education of the

[1] S. J. Curtis, *History of Education in Great Britain*, page 1.

Poor in the Principles of the Established Church'. This tells its own story. By the 1870 Education Act, the State first intervened effectively in English education by the setting up of School Boards, and establishment of the Dual system. Between 1870 and 1944, however, the positions of Church and State in education became gradually reversed. Whereas before 1870 the Churches had been proprietors, after 1944 they found themselves in the position of junior partners.

During this period the aims of religious education changed, as the basis of the educational system changed. Whereas before 1870 the aims were seen to be ecclesiastical—meeting the membership needs of the churches, after 1944 they were seen to be educational—meeting the spiritual needs of the children. This is made clear in Lord Butler's statement quoted in Chapter I, above: 'My general aim and intention in framing the clauses dealing with religious education in what became the Education Act of 1944 was to recognize formally this special place of religion in education.' This is supported by the remarks made by Archbishop Lord Fisher, and quoted by Professor Niblett in Chapter I, above. 'We have been assured by Lord Fisher that though most of the discussions which the delegation from the Protestant Churches had with Mr Butler related to the theological content of an agreed syllabus, their aims were educational, not ecclesiastical. "Willie Temple and I were both schoolmasters," he said, "that tells you all you need to know".'

This educational aim is re-emphasized in the first recommendation made by the conference.

The puzzled parent reading this report may well express surprise that the conference's first recommendation should be so obvious a restatement. The difficulty is that the aims of the administrators have not always been the aims of all the teachers and some confusion of thought has arisen from time to time on this issue. Many teachers of religious education, and particularly non-specialists, often do their work from strong religious motivations. Quite understandably, they may come to the classroom with strong ecclesiastical or evangelistic assumptions, and find an educational aim frustrating.

What is meant by an educational aim was simply if rather artlessly expressed by the conference member who said, 'The aim is surely to give children a core of knowledge and experience so they don't leave school ignorant of what Christianity stands for, but it is not the teacher's business to proselytize, but to present Christianity attractively so they can choose.' This is substantially what has been said by recent writers on the subject. 'The overall aim in religious education should be to seek to teach rather than to preach, to enlighten rather than to convert.'[1] Professor A. V. Murray has neatly expressed how extensive can be the scope of an educational aim:

> . . . Religious education in school has two aspects. It is an education in itself and there are . . . sound educational reasons why it should be a subject in every school. But it is also preparatory to the fullness of Christian experience, both personal and corporate. The challenge that is inherent in it is one which the teacher should neither give nor avoid. It is inherent in the subject matter properly taught, and to attempt to emphasize it apart from that subject matter is to go beyond purely educational requirements.[2]

Despite this, there are still some who misconceive this aim, especially if they have never learnt to think educationally. Some teachers, e.g. feel it their duty to present their pupils with 'full Church teaching', others with 'the whole Gospel', pressing them to commitment and conversion. In the County school, however, the religious instruction must be given in accordance with an agreed syllabus, and should positively express the theological standpoint implicit in the agreed syllabus. What may be regarded as appropriate teaching at an Anglo-Catholic Congress, or in Harringay arena, is inappropriate in the classroom of the county school. What a teacher

[1] F. H. Hilliard, *The Teacher and Religion*, James Clarke, page 47.
[2] A. V. Murray, *Education into Religion*, Nisbet, page 214.

wishes to do outside the classroom in church, youth club, or voluntary society is entirely another matter—there he may teach what he pleases and proselytize with complete freedom. What he may do in the classroom is, in the plainest terms, bounded by statutory limitations.

The objection may then be made that religious education is pointless, empty, unspiritual, that it is mere teaching about religion, not the teaching of religion itself. An educational aim for religious education neither requires nor implies this.

Two examples will suffice. Suppose a lesson is to be given on the subject of 'Biblical sites in Palestine'. In the hands of a poor teacher this would indeed by teaching 'about' religion, religious education at its dullest. But let us suppose that the lesson is taught by Trevor Huddleston, or George Macleod, or Donald Soper. What the pupils will *actually learn* from that lesson is something very far beyond the Biblical sites of Palestine. Or to take another example, drawn from the often arid and contentious world of the academic theologians. Professor D. M. Baillie was for twenty years Professor of Theology in the University of St Andrews. As a University teacher his aims were, of course, educational. In the lecture hall and classroom he sought to teach and to enlighten; at no time as a teacher did he conceive it his duty to proselytize or press for conversions. Yet this is what two of his pupils wrote of him:

> Many of us have travelled 5,000 miles to sit at his feet—we would gladly have travelled twice that distance. His teaching had that mark of profound simplicity which can only be the result of years of strenuous, careful study . . . yet his lectures were marked by gentleness, wit and piety. No question was too insignificant, no personal problem too unimportant for his concern. None of us ever discovered the boundary or depth of so great a heart.
>
> He was a saint in whose transparent humility we saw reflected the beauty of holiness.[1]

[1] J. Baillie, Biographical Essay in *The Theology of the Sacraments*, Faber, P.B.

The point surely is this: that the teaching of religion, whether in school or university is only as pointless, empty and unspiritual as the people who teach it, and the concepts of religion are not well communicated by dogmatic or emotional bludgeonings.

An educational aim for religious education is most commonly misconceived by those who have never paused fully to examine what it entails.

Nor does an educational aim for religious education imply any diminution of the influence of religious education in moral education, rather does it place it in its proper context. It is psychologically, sociologically, educationally and theologically naive to suppose that moral education can be limited to the teaching of religious education or any other specific subject. Rather is it a subtle, profound and many sided process which the whole school shares with many other social influences and in which the conscious discussion of specific moral issues plays an important but subsidiary part. In so far as the school is able to exert moral influence—and this is an important qualification in contemporary society—religious education has its part to play, as has the effective teaching of other school subjects. It will also be important in helping to create the whole 'ethos' which is probably the school's most profound influence in moral education. The point is that religious education in school is only *part* of the process of moral education and it cannot possibly be expected to carry the burden alone. Nor should the teaching of religion be seen to have its place in the school curriculum principally as a means of promoting moral improvement in society.

The committed Christian will also note that an educational aim for religious education in no way denies or prevents the possibility that Christian commitment and Church membership may result. Many young people, totally out of contact with the Churches, have in fact come to Church membership through their religious education. They did so, however, as a result of the exercise of their own conscious choice based on what they had learnt and discussed week by week, not as a result of ecclesiastical or emotional pressures.

In this first section I have been trying to establish three main points:

(a) That the aims of religious education under the 1944 Act are fundamentally educational.

(b) That an educational aim does not imply merely barren teaching 'about religion'.

(c) That the teaching of religion in the county schools must be seen to have its place in the curriculum for this basic educational aim, and not for aims which are secondary or derivative.

This report deals solely with religious education in the county schools maintained by the State. What the aims of religious education may be in Independent schools, or schools fully maintained by the Churches is, as will be realized, entirely another matter. The aims may there be educational, ecclesiastical or evangelistic, as the governing bodies of the schools concerned choose to decide.

The Statutory Arrangements for Religious Education

It would certainly seem that Mr Butler, as he then was, rightly judged the wishes of teachers, parents, Churchmen, and society at large when in 1944 religious education was made a statutory requirement. In recent years some have wondered if the opinions of society might have changed. The events of 1965 would suggest that they have not, to any substantial degree.

The second recommendation of the conference shows that the majority of members favoured the continuance of the existing statutory arrangements, and this recommendation is in accord with the views attributed to the majority of adults. The magazine *New Society* published the result of a National Opinion Poll survey on religious education in their issue of May 27, 1965. This revealed that the overwhelming majority were in favour of continuing the present arrangements.

o

As an index of probability, the main findings of the poll are of interest and may be briefly summarized:

To the question, 'What is your religion?'

    92·9% described themselves as Christian.

    1·1% described themselves as atheist or agnostic.

    1·8% described themselves as no religion.

To the question, 'Is Britain a Christian country?'

    79·7% answered Yes.

    19 % answered No.

To the question, 'Should the present arrangements for religious education in schools continue?'

    90 % answered Yes.

    8·3% answered No.

It is not made clear whether this 8.3 percent against is a vote against religious education as such, or against religious education under the 1944 arrangements. It may well include a percentage who seek to preserve religious education, but wish to see the 'compulsory' requirement removed.

Both the results of this poll and the vote of the conference suggest that, in society at large, repeal of the religious education clauses of the act is certainly not a live issue and that any attempt to exclude the teaching of religion from the schools would be vigorously contested. Politicians and administrators contemplating educational legislation will perhaps be well advised rightly to discern the signs of the times.

There are, however, no possible grounds for complacency. Repeal of the Act on this point may not be a live issue at present, but it could very well become so if the quality of religious education is not improved. Much valuable work is being done in many schools and it is the merest exaggeration to suggest that all the teachers of religious education are in a ferment of discontent. Nevertheless, as has been made abundantly clear in this report, very many reforms remain to be made if the teaching of religion is to continue as a live and effective option in the schools. Religious education will receive the legislation it deserves and the votes of adults will be of little avail if what happens in the classroom is irrelevant, incompetent, or untrue.

The Staffing Crisis

The third recommendation made by the conference goes to the heart of the problem. It is one thing to sit in the House of Commons and pass an Education Act; it is quite another to ensure that the necessary conditions exist to make the Act educationally effective. In 1944 a vast demand was created overnight for qualified teachers of religious education. At the same time, no effective steps were taken to ensure that an adequate supply would be forthcoming. Possibly officialdom still subscribed to the myth of 'simple Bible teaching'. But the theologians have shown us that the Bible is not a simple book, and the psychologists have shown us that religious education is not a simple process. An adequate supply of specialist teachers is the most elementary condition of any religious education which is to be worthy of the name.

The reports of all enquiries into religious education in schools since 1944 have repeatedly stressed the staffing problem. This was made clear in 1954 by the Institute of Christian Education's report *Religious Education in Schools*, and again in 1961 by the University of Sheffield Institute of Education report *Religious Education in Secondary Schools*. It was a fact well known by head teachers and by the inspectorate. It was emphasized again in 1965 by the joint enquiry undertaken by the National Union of Teachers and the Education Department of the British Council of Churches. It might reasonably be supposed that a fact so plain and so often repeated would have resulted in some effective joint action between the (then) Ministry of Education, the Churches, and the voluntary organizations.

The figures presented by Mr Ayerst in Chapter IV and by Dr Hilliard in Chapter VI above, stress yet again the existence of the problem, and illustrate the extent of its size and seriousness. If the teaching of chemistry, physics, or mathematics in secondary schools lay in the hands of teachers four-fifths of whom lacked any specialist qualifications, we should not be surprised to find it was said to be largely ineffective. Nor would we be surprised to see joint action being taken by industry, the universities, the Department of Education and Science, and the LEAS to remedy a situation so fraught with educational and economic peril. Why then do we seem to regard religious education as so different and less important?

This staffing crisis is part of a much wider problem, and will not easily or quickly be resolved. It is not necessary to reiterate again the many reasons which aggravate staffing difficulties in teaching, and which make the forecasting of staffing needs so problematic. Certainly, the specific staffing needs of religious education must be planned in the light of the national supply and demand for teachers of all kinds. (See *The Demand for and Supply of Teachers 1963-1986*, H.M.S.O. 1965.)

The members of the conference recommended the setting up of a joint executive body to enquire into this specific problem and act upon it. I am in complete agreement. Far too little is known about this whole subject. This body could, e.g.:

(a) Examine effective ways and means of encouraging young people to enter teaching, especially considering the need for religious education specialists at every level.

(b) Examine the adequacy of existing arrangements for the further training of serving teachers who wish to specialize in religious education

(c) Examine ways and means whereby more mature men and women may be encouraged to enter the teaching of religious education from other occupations, and what facilities exist for their training.

(d) See what use could be made of suitably qualified clergy and ministers either as full time or part time teachers, and what facilities exist for their training as teachers.

It is clear that action is required at national level without delay. Pious hope is no substitute for educational planning.

School Worship

Before 1944 it was a very widespread custom in British schools for the day to begin with a school assembly consisting of, e.g., a hymn, Bible reading, prayers, etc., the whole lasting ten to fifteen minutes. Under the 1944 Act this became not merely a customary act but a statutory requirement. Paragraph twenty-six also laid down that 'The collective worship . . . shall not in any county school, be distinctive of any particular religious denomination.'

Lord Butler is quoted in Chapter I above:

> I know that during the debates some doubts were expressed about the wisdom of making . . . the corporate act of worship a specific requirement of the Act (subject of course to the right of withdrawal). But these doubts sprang, I think, mainly from the thought that it was unnecessary to make compulsory something in this field which was in practice universal. . . .

It is clear from a study of Hansard for 1944 that a group of Members of Parliament expressed some uneasiness about the 'compulsory' requirement, and that their doubts sprang often from religious principle. Mr E. Harvey, MP, e.g., held that Parliament could say that schools should provide facilities for worship, but that the act of worship itself is an interior state and cannot be compelled.[1] Other MP's expressed similar reservations suggesting that the 'compulsory' requirement might in the long run militate against what worship is meant to express and achieve. An element of doubt is still apparent in contemporary educational thought on this question.[2]

The results of the National Opinion Poll survey published in May 1965, to which reference has already been made in this

[1] See Hansard, Vol. 397, page 2395.
[2] See Chapter One, above.

Chapter, gives no information on this specific issue. No distinction appears to have been made in the questionnaire between religious instruction and worship. It may be safe to infer that there is little desire in society at large for any alteration of the law on this point. The number of parents who withdraw their children from school assembly remains fractional, and the withdrawal is often for denominational reasons.

The members of the conference made clear by their fourth recommendation that they were divided on the question of whether or not the 'compulsory' requirement should be retained. A small majority appeared to feel that religious education might stand to gain more than it might lose if a greater degree of flexibility was to be allowed. This is a problem which only time and greater experience will resolve. What is significant is that the overwhelming majority of members were agreed that some facilities for school worship should continue to be provided, since worship is an integral part of religious education. Professor W. R. Niblett in Chapter VII of his *Christian Education in a Secular Society*[1] has suggested how school worship serves a double purpose. For the already committed Christian boy or girl it is expressive, if often unsatisfying; for the uncommitted it may be introductory. This 'educational' element of school worship was also stressed by Dr F. H. Hilliard in Chapter II of *Christianity in Education*.[2] The argument briefly is that worship is an integral part of the practice of religious education and young people can scarcely be expected to understand it unless they are allowed to experience it. It is important to realize that this is by no means a piece of special pleading but a direct application to the school situation of principles long established by liturgiologists. F. H. Brabant, e.g., in his section on 'The expressive and suggestive elements in worship', on page twelve of *Liturgy and Worship*[3] writes as follows:

[1] Oxford University Press, 1960.
[2] op. cit.
[3] ed. by W. K. Lowther Clarke, S.P.C.K.

All liturgical acts . . . have a double function : one directed God-wards, expressing in outward form the thoughts and feelings of the worshippers, the other directed manwards, teaching the worshippers how they ought to think and feel . . . worship, therefore has not only an expressive function, but also a suggestive or impressive one, these terms are far from being ideal . . .

We should prefer to speak of school worship as having both its expressive and its educational elements. For both these reasons it is evident that the quality of school worship is of the greatest importance, and on this score members of the conference expressed widespread dissatisfaction. It is unfortunately true that school assembly is too often a dreary travesty of worship, unimaginatively planned, poorly led, and taking place in cramped and squalid surroundings. It is, I would suggest, this which perplexes pupils rather more than the 'compulsory' requirement.

Much has been written on the subject of the conduct of school worship and I have no desire to repeat at length what has been often dealt with by others. My own observations would suggest, however, that it is worth while strongly emphasizing yet again the following five points:

(a) It is not essential and may be positively undesirable that the head teacher of a school shall invariably conduct morning assembly. Some head teachers are agnostics and should certainly not be expected regularly to conduct a religious service. Others may have considerable academic or administrative gifts, but be fatally dull when attempting to lead the worship of 600 young people. It is sometimes suggested that a head teacher's status may be impugned if he does not conduct the school's daily assembly. This is not the experience of the independent schools. Morning worship in the boys' public schools is usually conducted by the chaplain or divinity master. The headmaster may occasionally take part, but it is the exception rather than the rule for him to officiate daily. It is not recorded of any of the great headmasters that their boys held them in any less respect on this account. It may be desirable for the conduct of daily assembly to be shared among willing members of staff, and that pupils should assist wherever possible.

(b) The quality of all worship is profoundly influenced by the surroundings in which it takes place. In theory it is possible to worship God as easily in a school hall as in Salisbury Cathedral. Most people find that in practice this is not so. Most of the independent schools accept without question that worship should take place in a building set apart for the purpose; the administrators of the State system appear to regard this as a financial impossibility. The county schools often labour under very severe limitations in this respect. Head teachers should exercise the greatest possible care to ensure that their school worship takes place in surroundings calculated to help rather than to hinder their pupils. Unnecessary overcrowding is the most commonly observed fault.

(c) Those responsible for the conduct of school assembly should seek to ensure that the service has been properly prepared. That unhurried simplicity which makes for reverence in worship is, amongst other things, the fruit of meticulous preparation by the officiant. Lessons, hymns and prayers should be carefully chosen on a long term plan, and not in accordance with daily whim.

(d) The officiant at school assembly should be at all times audible, and should conduct the service with reverence and dignity. It may seem astonishing that so obvious a point requires to be stressed, but my own observations are not propitious. We should not long endure clergy who in the course of Church services were in the habit of cuffing those members of their congregations who displeased them, e.g., by not singing. Yet there are head teachers who permit themselves liberties of this kind in conducting assembly.

(e) A definite division must be made, and must be seen to be made, between school worship and the reading of lists of notices by the head teacher. A short period should be allowed before the service begins to allow staff and pupils to be still and recollect themselves. Many schools find it helpful to play appropriate music during this time. After the service there should be a similar break. Only then should the head teacher feel free to embark on administrative instructions to the school. Further comment on this large and important theme is impossible within the necessarily limited space of this report. There are encouraging signs that more attention is being given to this topic, e.g., the recent report by the University of Leeds Institute of Education, 'School Worship', edited by C. M. Jones. A very great deal more care and imaginative action is required by head teachers, LEA advisers, and senior religious education teachers on this whole problem. For the vast majority of young people in Britain, the school assembly is their only personal experience of worship. It should therefore be a more attractive and inspiring introduction to genuine worship than it would sometimes seem to be.

Revision of the Agreed Syllabuses

Agreed Syllabuses came into general use in the 1920s. Under the 1944 Act, religious instruction in the county schools must be given in accordance with an Agreed Syllabus and must not contain any instruction which is specifically denominational. The Standing Advisory Council on religious education in each Local Education Authority consists of representatives of the LEA, The Church of England, the Free Churches, and the teachers. One of the duties of the council is to present the LEA with an agreed syllabus suitable for the schools in its area. The council may either specifically draw up a syllabus, or may recommend the use of a syllabus drawn up by another LEA. An Agreed Syllabus should contain outline details of what religious instruction should be given at different ages, together with recommended lists of books, teaching aids, etc. The fifth recommendation of the conference was that the majority of existing syllabuses require radical revision both in form and content.

An Agreed Syllabus does serve a valuable purpose. It does, e.g., (a) help the religious education specialist in drawing up schemes of work, (b) provide very useful guidance for the non-specialist, (c) give some indication of the theological standpoint which the religious instruction should express. Revision of a syllabus is a complex procedure, involving theological, educational, psychological and sociological considerations. Assistance should be made available to Councils through the Christian Education Movement, and through the various university institutes of education. Councils should include teachers who are theologically literate and clergy with knowledge of both the theory *and* practice of education.

In the conference discussions on this subject, three expressions enjoyed a general currency : 'relevant', 'child-centred', and 'open-ended approach'. I believe we have to consider these with caution.

It is certainly undeniable that some biblical material is more relevant than others to the needs and interests of young people, e.g., St Matthew's Gospel as compared with the Book of Leviticus. Yet 'relevance' stems not only from the content of the material, but also from the manner in which it is presented. In deciding the content of an Agreed Syllabus, therefore it is necessary to consider carefully what constitutes 'relevance' in the classroom situation. It is perfectly possible to teach the Gospel of St Mark in a highly irrelevant way, and it is equally possible to teach the Minor Prophets in such a way as to reveal the continuing relevance of their teaching to our contemporary situation.

It may further be asked in what way religious education may be said to be 'child-centred' without becoming involved in a fundamental contradiction. A 'child-centred' physical education is possible, but a 'child-centred' religious education is no more possible than a man-centred theology. If by 'child-centred' is meant the adaptation and selection of material suitable to the age and interests of the pupils, then the term has meaning. But if in religious education we seek to teach only what is within the child's comprehension and experience, then by the very natures of both child and subject matter we pursue a delusion.

The term most widely used in discussion was, however, 'open-ended approach', and this deserves careful scrutiny. It is an Alice-in-Wonderland type of expression which may enjoy general appeal because it means something different to every-body. Religious education has in the past been undeniably influenced by the dogmatic certainties of an earlier age. '... Which Faith except every one do keep whole and undefiled; without doubt he shall perish everlastingly ...' The words of the Athanasian Creed contrast strangely with the New Theology. Religious education certainly cannot any longer be a simple catechetical process in which the Church provides the right questions for which it has the right answers. Nevertheless, Christian theology is not yet in such intellectual disarray that religious education need degenerate into mere hazy discussion, that 'exchange of mutual mystification' to which Professor Nineham refers. If by 'open-ended approach' is meant the critical, intelligent, and informed presentation of biblical and doctrinal material by the teacher, followed by frank and open discussion by the class, then this is no more than trained and qualified teachers of religious education have been doing for years. If, on the other hand, it implies teachers abandoning what Christian scholars have taught for centuries in favour of embarking with their pupils on 'voyages of uninhibited spiritual discovery', then we must needs judge the enterprise to be ill-advised. One of the main characteristics of young people is still ignorance, and to assert that neither Christian theology nor Christian morality have any longer anything definite to teach them is to exhibit a dangerously mistaken humility.

What, then might a new syllabus for the secondary school possibly be expected to contain? Space permits only the briefest and most tentative reference to the main points, and the selection is a personal one.

In the lower school, there is still an undoubted case for the teaching of that solid core of biblical and historical material which must provide the basis for all informed religious education in British schools. The main events and personalities of the Old Testament presented in their historical context and religious significance; the life, teaching and ministry of Christ presented with careful reference to the New Testament text; some selective study of the outstanding events and personalities of Church history, etc. The fullest use would be made of modern text-books, dramatic work, visual presentation, and audio-visual side of all kinds. This type of course could be extended for those pupils staying on to the upper school and sixth form.

With classes in the middle school containing a high proportion of school leavers, one would expect use to be made of the 'discussion method', as described by Mr Harold Loukes in his *Teenage Religion*.[1] Reference should be made to this work for further details.

In the upper school one might expect scope to be given for a very wide variety of courses, e.g., in the basic elements of Christian doctrine; religion and philosophy; religion and science; prayer, worship and mysticism; religious themes in music, art and literature; and comparative religion. Again with sixth form leavers one would expect to see the fullest use made of the discussion method, covering not only the moral, social, and vocational problems facing young people in the modern world, but also the ultimate questions of meaning and purpose which face all men. The teaching would be relevant insofar as it made clear that religion stems from human experience and in turn affects that experience. It would be child-centred insofar as it was sensitively and realistically graded to the needs, interests and capabilities of children at different stages. It would

[1] S.C.M. Press, 1961.

be open-ended insofar as it was intelligent, informed, non-dogmatic, and deeply charitable.

Many teachers regarding the Agreed Syllabus for their area as irrelevant, out of date, and inept have ceased to use it. With able teachers, this may sometimes be desirable; with the less competent, it may be disastrous. What is certain is that LEA's can hardly expect teachers to respect an Agreed Syllabus which has been allowed to ossify into a quasi-credal statement expressing the theological thought and educational practice of a previous generation.

Specialization in the Primary School

Young children of primary school age have often a disconcerting habit of asking deeply penetrating theological questions. They have an equally disconcerting capacity for being able to sense when they are being given answers which are inane or inadequate. No one who has ever taught young children will be surprised to read of the class who sought to ask, 'Where is he now?' after having watched Sir Winston Churchill's funeral on television. Giving answers to questions such as these which are sincere, theologically informed, and to some degree within the comprehension of children is a task which would tax the wits of many a professor.

In the majority of primary schools, religious education is taught by the class teacher along with most other subjects. Whether or not this principle is desirable, is of course a long standing debate. Most of these teachers have followed the basic divinity course in their training college, and Miss Parnaby in Chapter V above, has discussed some of the serious deficiencies of this type of course. Many members of the conference appeared to support Mr Ayerst's plea for a greater degree of specialization in the primary school. It seems evident that too many teachers in the primary school have received very inadequate preparation in theology and psychology for a task of great importance and deceptive simplicity. As has been already stressed, the Bible is not a simple book, and religious education is not a simple process, least of all in the primary school. Dr Lincoln Ralphs has rightly emphasized in Chapter II how fundamentally important qualities of character and personality are in the teacher, particularly at this stage, and with this point few would disagree. Sincerity and conviction are essential characteristics of all effective teachers of religious education. But they must be seen as complementary to, and not substitutes for, an intelligent and meaningful grasp of the subject. This applies at every stage in education, not merely in the secondary school. That teachers require to give religious instruction to young children provides no excuse for a training which is theologically childish. The sixth recommendation of the conference is very clear on this point.

It is very obvious that what children may attain in their school work is directly related to the quality and competence of their teachers. From what has been said in the previous paragraph it will come as no surprise to find that recent enquiries into the results of the religious education of children at primary school age suggest a disappointing picture. Dr R. W. Goldman, in his book *Religious Thinking from Childhood to Adolescence*,[1] gives the findings of a Piaget-type psychological enquiry undertaken to discover what children can comprehend about religious concepts, and at what age. The basic conclusion may possibly be said to be that Agreed Syllabuses attempt to teach too much too soon, and that much biblical material is incomprehensible to children below the age of thirteen. It is, of course, quite impossible in these brief comments to do justice to Dr Goldman's findings, and the reader should refer to the book itself. The child mind is not, however, a tabula rasa, and enquiries into the comprehension of religious concepts must surely be seen— amongst many other factors—in relation to the quality of teaching which has helped to form those concepts. As can be seen by the seventh recommendation, many members of the conference expressed their appreciation of Dr Goldman's

[1] Routledge and Kegan Paul, 1964.

work as a valuable initial contribution to an important field of enquiry. Examination of the discussion notes would, however, suggest that not all members were in agreement with the nature of his investigation, or his conclusions, and would welcome much more extensive research of this type.

Theological Qualifications

Those of us responsible for the professional training of theology graduates who wish to teach in secondary schools have on occasions inclined to despair when presented with pupils holding high academic qualifications, possessing a meticulous knowledge of the Hebrew text of the Book of Jonah, but blandly ignorant of the philosophy of religion, Christian ethics, or contemporary theology. When they came to conduct sixth form discussions they found themselves nonplussed, unable to deal with the very questions their pupils sought to raise. Mr Ayerst in Chapter IV has criticized the heavy linguistic and textual demands made by many university theology courses. Dr Hilliard in Chapter VI criticized the 'preoccupation in university departments of theology with questions of mainly historical and textual detail.' Professor Nineham in Chapter IX has analysed the historical origins of existing theological courses and commented on the changed nature of the contemporary situation. The members of the conference expressed their views in their eighth recommendation.

We are sometimes reminded that it is not the function of a university department of theology to give vocational instruction. This is a difficulty which the faculties of law and medicine seem not incapable of overcoming. We are again sometimes reminded that the function of the academic theologian is to pursue the academic study of theology. This is not at all in doubt. What is being questioned is the nature of what is at present held to constitute 'academic theology' in British Universities. Academic theologians holding University appointments are also teachers with responsibility not only to their subject but also to their students. The majority of theology graduates enter either the pastoral work of the Churches, or the teaching of religious education in schools. As far as the needs of teachers are concerned, too many university courses in theology provide a training which is irrelevant and inadequate. I am conscious that these are serious allegations, but they would not be made had they not arisen directly out of experience and observation. The Rev. David Jenkins says in his contribution to the Downside symposium *Theology and the University* :

> Theology will progress in her task only as she learns not to make terms but to face up to the terms laid upon her by the present state and attitude of the world. The more she takes on the form of the servant, the more will the Word of God be manifested to men. (Page 162.)

I may perhaps be forgiven for suggesting that 'the form of the servant' is not at present the most immediately apparent characteristic of many faculties of theology.

A teacher of religious education, especially in a grammar or comprehensive school, should have as far as his theological preparation is concerned, some effective grasp of biblical studies, Christian doctrine, Church history, the philosophy of religion, ethics, contemporary theological thought, and the comparative study of religions. How far it is possible to achieve this within the present three year degree course is only one of many questions raised by this statement. It is very much to be hoped that realistic and imaginative thought will be given to the content and structure of university theology courses. Many academic theologians are acutely conscious of this whole issue and have already initiated changes. The recent proposals, e.g., by the Faculty of Theology at Oxford are to be welcomed. It is quite certain that the student of theology in the 1960s can find many more profitable subjects over which to agonize than Davidson's *Hebrew Grammar*.

Generalizations on a theme so wide as this are notoriously perilous. It should be recognized, however, that the substance of these observations may also apply to the main divinity courses in some training colleges.

Plans are now being made to implement one of the proposals of the Robbins Report whereby a proportion of students in colleges of education will be enabled to obtain the degree of Bachelor of Education. Those responsible for planning the contents of B.Ed. courses for divinity specialists have here an important opportunity for imaginative action and initiative. It would be exceedingly unfortunate if the worst type of academic theology were to be grafted in to the B.Ed. course to satisfy what is called 'intellectual respectability'. The theological content of the B.Ed. course must obviously be academically demanding and require rigorous study. It must also be relevant to the teaching situation and this consideration must not be outweighed by nervous concern for what in the past was regarded as respectable by academic theologians long since entombed.

By their ninth recommendation the members of the conference pointed to another aspect of this problem—the failure of communication which exists between the work of theologians in universities and teachers of religious education in schools. A number of practical ways and means were suggested whereby contacts could be preserved. This recommendation is largely self explanatory and requires little comment. Professor Nineham has spoken in Chapter IX above, of the complexity of contemporary theological scholarship and the need for 'expert instruction'. This will be achieved only if teachers of religious education keep alive their own theological studies. Many other teachers seek to make up the inadequacies of their own original theological training. Certainly they may read the books which the theologians may publish, but there is still a valuable place for the stimulus of personal contact.

The quality of religious education in the schools has also a real influence on the numbers and quality of students who will seek to read theology at university. Exact research remains to be done, but experience in this Institute of Education

P

suggests that many theology graduates training to be teachers have been directly inspired to do so through the example of competent teachers of religious education by whom they have been taught in school. It may be inferred that incompetent teaching will have a correspondingly deterrent effect.

The Standpoint of the Secular Agnostic

This must be seen in its proper perspective. The secularist organizations assert that about 20 percent of the teachers are 'humanists', or, more correctly, secular agnostics. The National Opinion Poll survey already referred to gives the figure of 1.1 percent describing themselves as atheists or agnostics in society at large. The exact statistical figures can be questioned, but it may safely be asserted that the teaching profession contains a markedly higher proportion of agnostics than does society in general, and that on the subject of religious education they are vociferous out of all proportion to their numbers. They are also seriously divided on this whole issue, and it can be questioned if any one sufficiently agreed 'standpoint' has yet emerged. Of late the secularist organizations have pointed with satisfaction to the large numbers of students who support the 'humanist' organizations in the universities of Oxford and Cambridge. Those of us with personal knowledge of the student societies of those universities are, however, predisposed to approach with caution conclusions based on their transient fortunes. Even King David passed some of his early years among the Adullamites.

Mr Harold Pinter has recently protested about the 'brainwashing' of children by teachers of religious education, and how offensive this is to 'humanist' parents. It is very difficult indeed to see the force of objections such as these when all parents have a legal right, written into the Education Act, to withdraw their children completely from all religious instruction, and school worship. Society in no way inhibits or prevents them then giving their children what agnostic or materialist instruction they may choose. If parents do not withdraw their children from religious instruction, the most obvious assumption which presents itself is that they are not agnostics, and wish their children to receive it. In British democracy it is hardly reasonable for a small minority of agnostic parents to wish to deny this right to the large majority of other parents who are not agnostic. Some members of the conference recognized that misunderstandings may sometimes arise on this issue when schools fail to take sufficient care to inform the parents of their pupils what legal rights they possess to withdraw their children. The second subsidiary recommendation stresses the need for schools to take great care to ensure that parents are fully informed on this point.

It is, furthermore, being gratuitously offensive to describe religious education in British schools as 'brainwashing' or 'indoctrination'. This type of accusation is linguistically, psychologically and educationally false, enjoys extensive empirical disproof, and is used in a strangely emotional way by those professing to be rationalists.

Agnostic teachers sometimes protest that they work under professional handicaps within the present structure of British education. That they are obliged to pretend to be religious when they are not, and find it prudent to conceal their true allegiance in order to obtain promotion. Mr Ayerst in Chapter IV has described the 'myth of religious education given by a mass of unbelieving conscripts', and has pointed out how this dies hard. 'But myth it is as far as the county secondary school teachers are concerned . . . the great majority of those who give religious education in the county secondary schools do so because they want to, or because they think they ought to.' He stresses how little there is now to prevent secondary school teachers taking full advantage of the conscience clause. It is then, in appointment to headships that this difficulty may presumably most keenly be felt. But if we live in so 'open' a society as has been described to us in Chapter X, above, then it follows that the 'open-ness' will also extend to those men and women who are members of school governing bodies, and who are responsible for appointments. 'Pretence and concealment' are surely rather irrelevant notions in an 'open' society. If, however, we do not live in an 'open' society, but in a society which seeks a religious education for its children, then let none of us pretend or conceal the inevitable implications. My own personal view on this question is that discussions about pretence and concealment, withdrawal rights, opting in or opting out, and so on, are of limited usefulness, and may serve only to obscure the real problem which is the basic cleavage of fundamental principle. In former ages men built Churches, and the schools associated with those Churches, because they believed the knowledge, worship, and service of God to be man's primary concern. They taught Christianity in their schools because they believed it to be true, and because they believed the religious dimension of man's life be of absolute significance. The secular agnostic view is the categorical denial of this position. It enthrones man, not God, at the centre, classifies religion as outdated superstition, and looks to a future regulated by science and man's reason. Much discussion of the administrative arrangements for religious education is the projection of this conflict on to that part of the educational system most sensitive to it. Theologians and secular agnostics have much to learn from one another, and there is no doubt that dialogue between them should be continued. Christian educationalists and 'humanists' should likewise meet to discuss matters of common concern, such as moral education, and to ensure that the administrative arrangements for religious education represent the fairest possible expression of the prevailing situation. The type of religious education which exists in a society appears, however, to be very largely conditioned by historical circumstances. The real question at issue is not so much whether or not religious education shall be given in schools as whether or not the educational system shall be based on principles which are religious, or principles which are secularist and materialistic. This, in turn, depends on the outcome of that conflict of belief which lies at the very heart of the whole of our contemporary culture, and which it may take centuries to resolve. The secular agnostic believes that rationalism will eventually supervene and that Christianity together with other world religions will be relegated to mythology. The Christian seems to have heard this too often before to be greatly disposed to believe it. What is important is that religious education should be seen in this full perspective and total dimension, and never merely as an issue between two squabbling educational pressure groups.

By their tenth recommendation the members of the conference expressed themselves on the whole willing to discuss the agnostic viewpoint when it arose, but unwilling positively to introduce into the curriculum teaching which they believed to be untrue.

A National Association of Teachers of Religious Education

By their thirteenth recommendation, members of the conference expressed support for the view that a professional organization should be established for teachers of religious education. This body could, e.g., represent their professional interests, make policy statements, organize courses and conferences at national and local level, and so on. In the past, the Institute of Christian Education attempted to fulfil this function. As has already been stated in the Introduction, this body has now been merged with the Student Christian Movement in Schools, the YMCA, and the YWCA to form the Christian Education Movement. What may have been in the minds of the members of the conference who expressed themselves on this issue is an uneasiness that the wider aims of the Christian Education Movement are not wholly compatible with the particular needs of a professional association. It may well be that a division or department of the Christian Education Movement could be established to meet this need.

Local Education Authority Advisers on Religious Education

The first subsidiary recommendation urges Local Education Authorities to appoint full time advisers on religious education.

At present, only two LEAS have done so. This recommendation arose spontaneously out of discussion in three out of the five groups, and deserves serious consideration.

The LEA Adviser on religious education has a task of great importance and difficulty. He might well be expected to:

(a) Assist and advise teachers and head teachers in schools of all kinds on all questions relating to religious instruction and school worship, including the provision of text books and teaching aids.

(b) Organize regular courses at local centres for teachers, school leavers, parents, and others.

(c) Liaise with representatives of the local churches, voluntary organizations, diocesan directors of education, and so on.

(d) Advise the local education authority as a member of the standing advisory council on all questions relating to religious education.

It is clear that anyone appointed to this work would have to possess uncommon ability, and to have very large reserves of tact, patience and charity. The right person could perform a very real and important service; the wrong one could have a most seriously divisive and disrupting influence.

Training Methods in University Departments of Education

At present, the theology graduate who seeks to train as a specialist teacher of religious education in a secondary school normally does a one year full time course in a university department of education. Dr Hilliard in Chapter VI, above, has outlined the structure of one such course, and it is unnecessary to repeat the details. The fourth subsidiary recommendation suggests that some enquiry is necessary into the effectiveness of the training methods used in these courses. Those of us who work in this field will not be surprised by the recommendation. The inadequacies of existing courses and the serious questions they provoke have been discussed for some years. In these brief comments it is possible only to repeat a few of the more obvious questions.

Is there a basic difference in kind between the training of a graduate teacher of religious education and, say a teacher of physics? Is a one year course consisting of teaching practice together with some introduction to the philosophy, psychology, sociology and history of education anything like relevant to the particular needs of the theology graduate taking responsibility for religious education in the secondary school? Is a training which is academic and methodological adequate for one who seeks to communicate concepts which are basically spiritual? Is a period in some non-academic work such as Voluntary Service Overseas, or in industry, essential rather than desirable for teachers of religious education—particularly men—when their own maturity and experience of life is so important? Is the purpose of the training year not so much to instil educational theory as to give students some opportunity to digest the large lumps of often very undigestible academic theology they have swallowed in haste at the University—to provide an opportunity for personal synthesis before being subjected to the questionings of sixth formers? What attempts should be made to remedy the often very serious inadequacies in the students' theological preparation, e.g. in ethics and the philosophy of religion?

These are only a few of many possible questions. It is clear that they have to be considered within the context of over-all policy for graduate teacher training. This, in turn, raises yet more questions. It is, however, apparent that the training of graduate teachers of religious education is a subject fraught with its own particular problems, and one meriting more thought and enquiry. This might well possibly form the theme of a separate study conference by the Lecturers responsible for the teaching of religious education in the University Departments of Education.

Relations between the Schools and the Churches

This section touches on a very much larger theme—the whole question of the Churches' part in education. What the func-

tion of the Churches should be in the rapidly changing structure of British education is a problem so important, so complex
and many-sided, that a completely separate enquiry will be
necessary. Initial plans are already being prepared for a study
conference on this subject. At this stage it is only possible to
make very brief comments which may well be of an interim
nature.

Reliable statistics on this point are difficult to find. Nevertheless, it would be realistic to assert that at present no more
than 10 percent of young people of school age are in effective,
regular, personal contact with the Churches. By this is meant
attendance at confirmation classes, or other similar courses leading to full membership. Attendance at open youth clubs, coffee
bars, etc. can scarcely be regarded as valid in making this
assessment. The exact percentage figure may be argued. What
cannot be doubted is that whereas only a very small proportion
of young people are in effective, regular, personal contact
with the Churches, all (except the fractional minority withdrawn by their parents) receive religious education in their
schools. As has already been made clear in the first section of
this report, the aim of religious education in the school is
neither to proselytize nor to convert. Yet it is obvious that
the influence of religious education in the schools is of quite
fundamental importance in creating the whole climate of attitude and outlook in which the Churches have to do their work.
It is from teachers of religious education—not from the clergy
—that the vast majority of young people in Britain receive their
only personal Christian teaching and example. It is in the
schools—not in the Churches—that they receive their only
personal experience of worship. The Churches continue to
neglect what happens in religious education to their own serious
loss. There are a few leaders of the Churches who realize this
point very clearly indeed and are prepared to face its implications. There are too many upon whom this fact, even after
twenty years, appears not yet to have impinged. Bishop Hensley Henson once wrote:

Instead of this incessant prating about a 'Way of Renewal', and a multiplying of . . . the Lord only knows what other latter day quackeries which may distract us from our obvious duties, what we want is nothing more than an honest pedestrian fidelity to pledged and acknowledged obligations.[1]

The Churches will do well to heed his words. Parish work and education are the two principal means whereby the Churches have served the needs of men, women, and children for 2,000 years. In the confusion of thought and practice which seems to afflict the contemporary Church there is real danger that obvious truths of this kind may be submerged.

The eleventh recommendation of the conference stressed the need for closer relationships between the schools and the Churches. What may be done at local level to achieve this has been helpfully dealt with by the Rev. J. A. Wainwright, Secretary of the Education Department of the British Council of Churches, in his book *School and Church*.[2] 'With the development of the ecumenical movement,' he writes, 'Churches have grown very much closer together. Many teachers are finding that they are showing themselves worthy of their confidence. As a result, during the past fifteen years or so there has been a growing movement to think of schools and churches as partners in the field of education, co-operating for the benefit of children.' Mr Wainwright discusses the educational principles which should guide planning, and provides a number of practical suggestions. What may be done, e.g., by local Churches to assist teachers of religious education in the schools; what the Churches may do for interested pupils who seek to supplement and extend the religious instruction they have received at school, and so on. Head and assistant teachers, parish clergy, parents, and members of local Councils of Churches will be

[1] E. F. Braley, ed., *More letters of Herbert Hensley Henson*, S.P.C.K., 1954, page 72.
[2] Oxford University Press, 1963.

well advised to study this book in the light of their own local situation, and take what action may be possible. It is depressingly obvious that nothing like sufficient imaginative thought is being given at local level to this important and difficult problem. The recent initiative by the Archbishop of York is to be welcomed. In May 1965 he appointed a commission of teachers and clergy under the Chairmanship of the Hon Richard Wood, MP 'to consider the problems of teachers and pupils with reference to religious worship and religious instruction in county and voluntary schools within the Diocese of York, and to report.' It is very much to be hoped that other local Church leaders will take similar action.

Sunday Schools

The need to improve the quality of teaching in Church Sunday schools was stressed in the conference's twelfth recommendation. Some members commented on the confusing effect which inferior or contradictory Sunday school teaching could have, particularly on religious education in the junior school.

In *Facts and Figures about the Church of England* published by the Church Information Office, 1962, the steady decline in Sunday school attendance figures in England was correlated graphically with the steady increase in figures for car ownership (diagram XXIII). This apparent correlation might provide some negative satisfaction but for the fact that the situation which prevails in the United States of America is the exact opposite. Sunday school membership figures there have continued to rise as car ownership has risen. The reason for this is not hard to find. In the American Churches, 'Christian education' is a matter of major concern, involving full time organizers, special buildings, and high quality literature. In the British Churches, the Sunday school, where one exists, is all too often a genial confusion presided over by well intentioned but untrained layfolk. Children cannot be expected to take seriously surroundings and instruction markedly inferior to that to which they are accustomed in their day schools. It is clear that a re-examination of the whole place and function of the Sunday school is required. Instruction given in Sunday school should obviously be planned in relation to the instruction which the pupils will receive in their day schools. It may, however, seriously be questioned whether the traditional Sunday school pattern has continuing relevance in the present educational and pastoral situation. This problem falls outside the scope of this report, but is by no means new and merits careful examination by the appropriate ecclesiastical authorities.

Employment of Clergy and Ministers as Teachers in County Schools

The employment of clergy and ministers as teachers in county schools is both legally permissible and common practice. No reliable statistics which may be authoritatively quoted have been made available, but it is evident from the comments of H.M.Is., head teachers and Church leaders that large numbers of clergy and ministers have moved in recent years into full time teaching. These men are appointed to schools on their academic status as graduates not on their ecclesiastical status as clergy. As an infusion of manpower they represent a useful addition to the teaching force. What this may imply for the future of the parochial system and the Free Churches is another matter.

Unfortunately—both for themselves and for their pupils—many of these men fail to realize that the techniques and assumptions of the pulpit are emphatically not those of the classroom. The sixth subsidiary recommendation of the conference states that clergy entering teaching must be trained as teachers.

Suitably qualified clergy proposing to make teaching their permanent occupation should naturally pursue a year's course of postgraduate training and obtain the Postgraduate Certificate or Diploma in Education in common with other graduates.

The necessary financial grants are available from the Department of Education and Science.

Those proposing to teach part time, or for only a part of their ministry should attend short courses organized by the Education departments of the Churches for this purpose. The recent initiative by the Bishop of London is to be welcomed. A short course organized by the Diocesan Director of Education is to take place annually in London for clergy wishing to teach in Church or county schools. Opportunities will be given for supervised teaching practice, and instruction in method provided by staff from the Church of England Board of Education, and the University Institute of Education.

Non-graduate clergy who seek to enter teaching are normally required to write directly to the Department of Education and Science who then recommend a course at a specific training college.

Clergy and ministers may sometimes bring much experience, learning and insight into the classroom. Nevertheless the fact remains that a theological college course was never intended to be a preparation for school teaching. Religious education has suffered too much too long from the well meaning efforts of incompetent amateurs, both clerical and lay.

Religious Education in the Theological Colleges

The conference's seventh subsidiary recommendation stressed that ordinands in the Church of England and the Free Churches should receive more serious preparation in the principles and methods of religious education.

All that has been stated hitherto in this report serves to illustrate the importance of religious education for the whole life and work of the Churches. Commonsense alone would require that ordinands should have an informed knowledge of the subject. Some theological colleges already provide a 'teaching week' for their students. Talks are given on classroom method, visual aids, etc., with particular reference to the junior school. Those responsible for conducting such courses would be the first to stress their necessarily limited aims. A 'teaching week' of the existing pattern is wholly inadequate for any serious presentation of the principles, aims and methods of religious education in the county schools. Some members of the conference expressed surprise that there was not more local co-operation between the theological colleges, university departments of education, and training colleges. The already crowded nature of theological college courses is recognized. It remains, however, inexcusable that so little attention is paid to a subject of such obvious practical relevance.

There is a further reason why this subject should receive more attention in theological education. Dr Hilliard in Chapter VI, above, has stressed the staffing crisis in religious education and has suggested what the annual intake of theology graduates into teaching should be if religious education is to remain a live option, particularly in the grammar and comprehensive schools. This must primarily be seen as one of the most important fields of service for qualified lay people. But, as was observed in the previous section, increasing numbers of clergy and ministers are being employed as either full-time or part time teachers. In the present situation of rapid educational expansion there is no doubt that this is a tendency which will increase, particularly in the case of clergy and ministers who are graduates. It is no exaggeration to say that the educational system could, under present conditions, absorb all those with relevant qualifications who wished to enter it. The future implications of this may well be very serious indeed for the Churches and deserves the most careful enquiry by those responsible for the training and deployment of the clergy.

Conclusion

The shortcomings of this report are obvious. Many subjects have necessarily had to be omitted. Too little has been said about the implications of the conference recommendations—it is no exaggeration to say that separate books could have been written about each one of them. What a symposium may gain through the wide experience and ability of its contributors it may lose in inner unity and coherence. Nevertheless, some of the main needs of religious education in the foreseeable future have been made very plain.

As was made clear in the Introduction, this report expresses the opinions of a number of able men and women who are engaged in the day to day work of religious education, and who care about it very deeply indeed. It is a group which flatly refuses to abandon future generations of British children to the fatuities of secularism, still less to the bleak negations of 'the humanist alternative'. It is a group which believes that the spiritual dimension in man's life matters, and that therefore religious education matters.

Changes do not take place overnight in British Education. Religious education has a very ancient lineage in our culture and will be neither lightly nor quickly removed from the curriculum of British schools. In 1944 it was given a place of special significance in our educational structure. Nothing like sufficient action has been taken over the past twenty years to ensure those conditions which make for educational effectiveness in this subject. We are now at the parting of the ways. No greater disservice could be done to religion in this country than that religious education in schools should be the half-hearted communication of half-comprehended half-truths by the half-trained to the half-interested. If religious education should ever cease to have a place in British schools it will not be through the nervous agitations of agnostics. It will be through the apathy, faithlessness, timidity, triviality and sheer incompetence of those for whom it is a professional responsibility.

GEORGE ALLEN & UNWIN LTD

London: 40 Museum Street, W.C.1

Auckland: Box 36013, Northcote Central, N4
Bombay: 15 Graham Road, Ballard Estate, Bombay 1
Bridgetown: P.O. Box 222
Buenos Aires: Escritorio 454-459, Florida 165
Calcutta: 17 Chittaranjan Avenue, Calcutta 13
Cape Town: 68 Shortmarket Street
Hong Kong: 44 Mody Road, Kowloon
Ibadan: P.O. Box 62
Karachi: Karachi Chambers, McLeod Road
Madras: Mohan Mansions, 38c Mount Road, Madras 6
Mexico: Villalongin 32-10, Piso, Mexico 5, D.F.
Nairobi: P.O. Box 4536
New Delhi: 13-14 Asaf Ali Road, New Delhi 1
Ontario: 81 Curlew Drive, Don Mills
São Paulo: Caixa Postal 8675
Singapore: 36c Prinsep Street, Singapore 7
Sydney, N.S.W.: Bradbury House, 55 York Street
Tokyo: 10 Kanda-Ogawamachi, 3-Chome, Chiyoda-Ku

THE BUDDHA, THE PROPHET
AND THE CHRIST

F. H. HILLIARD

It is often assumed that though the New Testament contains passages in which Christ is spoken of as divine, the sacred scriptures of Buddhism and Islam reflect only the belief that Gautama and Muhammad were but human religious teachers. This is by no means the case. In each of these scriptures also are to be found traces of a belief that the Founder of Buddhism or Islam manifested in his person and in his acts certain supernatural characteristics.

It is the main purpose of this book to bring together from the canonical writings of all these three great religions the most important of the passages in which this view of the Founder is reflected. The aim has been to let each of the sacred traditions tell its own story and only such comments have been added as seem necessary to bring out the full significance of the passage quoted. In a final chapter the author summarises some of the difficult questions which arise from a comparison of these extracts from the three traditions.   *Cr. 8vo.   About 12s. 6d. net*

THE CASTLE AND THE FIELD

AN ESSAY IN THE PSYCHOLOGY OF RELIGION

HAROLD LOUKES

This essay sets out to discuss the Quaker position in regard to the naturalist view of personality: the release from the conflict of conscience by the initial experience of the Inward Light; the means whereby personality was nurtured in the quiet generations that followed; and the moral situation in which Friends are placed by the withering of their old habits and the weakening of some of their testimonies.
Crown 8vo.   96 pages.   4s. 6d. paper.   6s. cloth

GEORGE ALLEN & UNWIN LTD